Praising Boys Well

**Other books available from Da Capo Press
by Elizabeth Hartley-Brewer**

Praising Girls Well

Talking to Tweens

Raising a Self-Starter

Raising Confident Boys

Raising Confident Girls

Raising Happy Kids

Praising Boys Well

100 Tips for Parents and Teachers

ELIZABETH HARTLEY-BREWER

Da Capo
LIFE LONG

A Member of the
Perseus Books Group

*For Richard, with deep thanks for
his love and unswerving support*

———————

Set in 10-point Stone Serif by the Perseus Books Group

Library of Congress Cataloging-in-Publication Data

Hartley-Brewer, Elizabeth.
    Praising boys well : 100 tips for parents and teachers / Elizabeth
Hartley-Brewer. — 1st ed.
        p.   cm.
    ISBN-13: 978-0-7382-1021-6 (pbk. : alk. paper)
    ISBN-10: 0-7382-1021-8 (pbk. : alk. paper) 1. Boys. 2. Praise.
3. Child rearing. 4. Self-esteem in children. 5. Parent and child.
6. Teacher-student relationships. I. Title.
HQ775.H33 2006
649'.132—dc22   2005028285

First Da Capo Press edition 2006

Published by Da Capo Press
A Member of the Perseus Books Group
http://www.dacapopress.com

Da Capo Press books are available at special discounts for
bulk purchases in the U.S. by corporations, institutions,
and other organizations. For more information, please contact the
Special Markets Department at the Perseus Books Group,
11 Cambridge Center, Cambridge, MA 02142, or call
(800) 255-1514 or (617) 252-5298, or
e-mail special.markets@perseusbooks.com.

1 2 3 4 5 6 7 8 9—09 08 07 06

Contents

Introduction

This book is for parents with boys of any age—babies, toddlers, or teenagers—and for teachers. Most of the tips can be used generally with any boy, but several relate to particular stages of development and show how our praise style should change as our boys grow. One of the most important lessons we have learned over the last two to three decades is how much children, regardless of their age, benefit from receiving praise from parents and teachers. Children respond far better to positive feedback and encouragement than they do to threats, criticism, and punishment. Many parents and teachers once found what they felt to be flattering words hard to use, especially with boys, and although some still find it hard, most people are now sufficiently familiar and comfortable with common phrases to give praise in good measure.

Praise has been viewed as the way to boost children's self-esteem, and to help them feel confident, and to fulfill their potential and be at ease with themselves. Many don't realize that using praise also has wider benefits for individual children and for society, because it can help to encourage self-discipline and moral behavior. However, nothing about parenting or children is straightforward. Boys, for example, often react to praise in different ways from girls and need their confidence reinforced in different areas. We are also beginning to realize that if praise is overused, used for particular personal motives, or directed at the wrong kind of activity, it may actually be unhelpful. When praise is overused or overhyped or belies the truth, boys may either become praise-dependent and require constant affirmation and approval or become indifferent to praise. Another possibility is that they may start to mistrust either the message or the messenger, wasting everyone's breath, or they might come to think they're superclever and special and annoy people with their self-importance, when in truth they're simply normal. Boys in particular can also feel swamped and suffocated by what they can experience as a continuous positive or negative commentary on their every move and are inclined to act out against the microscopic attention and constant judgment.

In addition, there is growing concern that overexposure to praise has led to children being ruined by rewards, dulled by "dumbing down," incapacitated by anxiety, or, at the very least, easily wrong-footed when faced with real challenges. They may then hide their anxiety with diversionary displays of daring and bravado in other spheres. And there's the worry that boys might be softened by pampering. For praise to be reliably effective, we have to be careful to understand fully its pros and cons, its wider value, and the approaches that are safest given boys' particular sensitivities.

This is what this book sets out to achieve. The early chapters (1–6) present the basic principles, tactics, and purposes. Chapter 1 develops an understanding of praise that underpins the thinking behind the one hundred tips that are spread equally among the remaining ten chapters. Chapter 4 enables readers to reflect upon the important features of child development and so relate the principles and tactics to the age and developmental stage of any particular boy. The later chapters (7–10) consider the subtleties and potential dangers of praise, and Chaper 11, the final chapter, invites the reader to self-reflect. Each tip stands alone and can be dipped into at random, but readers may like to read at least the introduction to each chapter in turn to gain an initial overview. This is a book to revisit on many occasions.

To show what this book covers, here are some questions and possible answers to consider. Think about why the different responses could matter.

When your son does particularly well, which might you say?

- "I'm really proud of you for managing that!"
- "I hope you feel proud of yourself—you should."
- "You probably feel really proud to have achieved that."
- "I feel so proud of you and proud that you're my child."

If your son makes the school soccer team, would you . . . ?

- Say, "Great! How many others tried out for how many places?"
- Promise to continue trips to the soccer field or park to develop his skills further.
- Go as a family to every match to give him support.
- Attend yourself and shout encouragement from the sideline.

*When your son tidies his room without being told,
would you . . . ?*

- Give him a hug and bring him a treat to eat.
- Say thanks, but laugh and say you wonder how long it will last.
- Give him money and hope this will persuade him to carry on the good work.
- Comment favorably on the improvement and ask what triggered the idea.

As you will discover in this book, praising well is a subtle art, and the way in which you phrase it can make a huge difference in whether a child feels freed and encouraged by your comments or, despite your good intentions, becomes anxious or angry because he senses a pressure to do even better. As you read through the one hundred tips that follow, you will come to appreciate the benefit of beginning most of your comments with *you* rather than *I*; of encouraging your son to judge his own efforts rather than rely on your view; of not taking any credit for his success; and of focusing on his reasons for and feelings about doing well, not yours.

Now read on!

Praising Boys Well

Chapter 1

Understanding Praise and How Boys React to It

Children love praise; of course they do, for most of us thrive on compliments and appreciation. Despite the pleasure it gives, children should be praised for more than just the delight praise brings them or the help it gives them to try harder. Praise needs to be a central part of raising children because it meets most of their fundamental needs. In other words, praise is not merely a bit of luxury, some additional fancy wrapping that we can leave out if we prefer. Children need to feel important and significant to someone, to believe that someone cares enough to cherish them, and this is at least as important as being properly fed and clothed. Children need to feel secure and to trust and rely on that care, which they can when they feel valued and central to their carer's life. They also need friendly and warm guidance, support, and direction about how they should lead their lives, so they need to hear what it is they should do rather than how they constantly fall short and disappoint. And in order for children to flourish, they need to know and be told they are capable, are enjoyed, and make others happy—particularly their parents.

Praise tends to be thought of as something spoken, put into words, but we can convey our pleasure, approval, and appreciation in many ways. Hugs, smiles, rewards, and touches, as we see in Chapter 6, all have their part to play and can sometimes be more effective because they can be more spontaneous and more direct. Even the spoken vocabulary of praise is more varied than at first appears, for the term *praise* includes many types of phrases and expressions that convey approval, appreciation, acknowledgment, and pure delight. The differences are important, as will become clear as the tips are explored.

It is deeply frustrating to realize that not all praise is helpful: Just when we thought we were getting it right, people are saying we could be getting it wrong. The good news is that it is not complicated to work out which styles and phrases are likely to support achievement and which sentiments can become confusing or burdensome and could cause problems. Effective relationships are always those that manage to keep a range of needs, styles, and goals in balance. The essence of constructive praise is that it is useful and encouraging: It provides relevant, detailed information; it is believable, so it is neither hollow nor false; and it may also show the way forward. Most important, the child should remain in full charge of his progress and be given opportunities to become confident in his ability to judge things for himself.

The energy that enables boys to take advantage of opportunity is self-belief. Self-belief is fueled when boys feel genuinely capable because they know in detail what it was they did right (which means they know they can do it again), because they have acknowledged the mistakes they made in the past and now know how to avoid them (which means failures have been faced, not ignored), and because they feel certain that they are unconditionally loved and accepted for who they are, not for matching up to someone else's ideal or for something they're especially good at. It is rarely helpful to celebrate every success and ignore every failure. Just as certain types of praise can be unhelpful, criticism can be constructive—when mistakes are acknowledged, identified, and ironed out, and the adjustments required are made clear.

Boys do need affirmation and acknowledgment as much as girls, but given the peer pressure, among older boys especially, to be "cool," to achieve without apparently trying, any praise or reward needs to be offered discreetly and with minimum fuss. Boys are not only readily embarrassed by overt praise (whether given in front of others or in private), but they are also more suspicious of it than girls. They are more inclined to feel potentially manipulated by praise and to accept it less willingly because they detect an ulterior motive.

When given to older boys, praise needs to be either matter of fact—very descriptive of what has been achieved—or short. Young men tend to clothe themselves in confidence, sometimes to a degree that masks an underlying fear of failure. When boys fail to deliver what's expected, it is often because they have been cavalier about the amount of preparation that was necessary and so aren't able to perform. In this event, the most useful response is to encourage them to look in detail at what they did not manage well so they understand what they need to do next time. They should not be allowed to hide behind some generalized assertion that it will be okay next time because they'll concentrate better, have a different teacher, or start to knuckle down sooner.

Boys need to be overtly valued by adult males, their fathers especially. From the age of about eight, boys typically begin to dismiss girls and other females and increasingly challenge their mothers and female teachers as they explore their male identity and assert their masculinity. Female approval may have less value and impact in their eyes than male approval. But many fathers find it hard to praise their sons, for fear of making them "soft" among other reasons.

Boys of all ages, but particularly younger boys, can find it quite hard to concentrate and apply themselves. "Stickability" is their big weakness. They are very easily bored, diverted, and distracted. In order to encourage boys to stay committed and focused, all positive feedback needs to be served up a little and often but always discreetly. If we wait until the end of whatever it is they're supposed to be working on, it could be too late; they may have lost the thread long before.

Boys need to be encouraged to become better organized and to plan ahead more effectively. They may need incentives and rewards to help them attend to their work. But being generally more attuned to power, boys are quick to bargain over the rewards offered and soon try to twist them to their advantage. Boys will need to be encouraged and admired for their personal qualities that show caring and sharing, friendship and reliability, not simply their strength or tactics that ensure success.

Chapter 2

The Purpose of Praise

What is praise for? It may seem an unnecessary question to ask, but it is important to be clear about what it is we are trying to achieve to help us check whether what we say and do is all-around beneficial with no negative side effects. For example, of course parents want to help their son grow up with good self-esteem: Self-esteem and strong self-belief are, indeed, valuable attributes, but their value is undermined if they come at the expense of sound self-knowledge (because he is told he's wonderful at everything), sound friendships (because friends are put off by his resulting bossiness and arrogance), and determination and perseverance (because he has never had to face and overcome setbacks). Parents can encourage the development of a boy's moral awareness by helping him to notice other people's helpful behavior and commenting favorably on their thoughtfulness, but if piling on praise leads to self-obsession and overconfidence, a boy's awareness of his impact on other people could be dulled. In order to decide whether our affirmative comments and actions are overall helpful, we should acknowledge the full range of possible desirable goals and the different categories and styles of positive feedback.

Here are some terms that help us to focus on the varied, deeper purposes of praise beyond the obvious ones: affirm, appreciate, approve, admire, attend, anticipate, achieve, acknowledge, be aware and alert, aspiration.

Each of these ten simple objectives is explored as a separate tip in this chapter.

It is useful to consider praise in terms of time zones. Although each encounter and incident is in the present, a key purpose of praise—and of support and encouragement—is to help our boys feel optimistic about their future, comfortable with the route they have traveled from the past, and content with the present. When we *encourage* them, our focus is on the future: We try to convince any boy in our care he will overcome any current difficulty to be successful hereafter. We therefore generate faith, hope, and confidence and give him heart. When we clearly *enjoy* his company and his achievements, we indicate our happiness and pleasure with who he is, in the present moment. When we *endorse* his actions, his view of the world, his approaches to learning, and his feelings, we are accepting those bits of him that have been fashioned by his past. If boys are comfortable about their past behavior and experiences, even if these were difficult, they are better able to look optimistically at the future. It is not helpful for parents or significant others to make a boy feel either ashamed of or guilty about his past or to dismiss it in an attempt to refocus and start again.

1   Affirm—to help him feel strong

Q: *If parents don't praise you directly, how else might you know that they're pleased with you?*

A: *When they leave me alone and let me get on with things without nagging me.*

—Alex, age 16

A: *When they give me more responsibility, it shows they trust me. That gives me a buzz and is like praise.*

—Mark, age 15

To affirm a child is to make a clear statement that confirms and accepts who he is. The word has its origins in a Latin word that means "strong." It therefore implies strength. When we affirm a child, we offer a firm statement of strong support, but it also gives children strength when they hear it.

To affirm is to make a neutral, judgment-free statement. Its essence is descriptive. The power and value of affirmation lie in its ability to encompass the past, present, and future—to endorse and encourage. We do not have to wait for any particular event or achievement to speak out. We can help our son to understand who he is at any time by describing what we see—his qualities and personality, his likes and dislikes, his particular talents—and then confirm how much we enjoy him as he is.

Parents	Teachers

- Think of ways to describe him and how he thinks and does things that will make him feel confident and strong inside.

  —"I love the way your eyes crinkle at the edges when you laugh."

  —"I've noticed how well you organized the ball game in the park, which makes me think you're responsible enough to go to the mall with your friends on the weekend."

- Ask him to help you with tasks either because he is good company or because he's good at that sort of thing.

- "I like your ideas and what you are trying to say. They'd be clearer and more powerful if you separated them. Try writing each idea down and thinking how each links to the rest."

- "Of course you will be upset that Carl is using the computer before you, but alphabetical order is what the class agreed on."

2 | Appreciate his achievements

For a young child, every day brings fresh challenges and fresh achievements. One day he can't do something, yet the next he can. Life is a growing experience in which more becomes manageable so competence can blossom. These achievements become the expression of being, and it is essential that they be fully appreciated.

One of the meanings of *appreciate* is "to be sensitive to." That is a significant definition. It suggests we should be sufficiently sensitive to see things on his level and in his terms: in relation to his challenges and difficulties, his limitations and capabilities, not our expectations.

Appreciation also includes the notion of value increasing, as in the value of houses or other forms of saving. Each child can be viewed as our most valuable asset. He will see that he goes up in your estimation each time you appreciate him and what he has managed to achieve. Of course, you love him, too, and he remains as important to you as ever, but every child really flies if he feels that those on whom he relies and whom he loves to the bottom of his being believe he has the potential to develop and impress.

Parents	Teachers

- "Achievement" can be very widely interpreted: Any advance in reading level, sociability, confidence, math computation, height and reach, ball skills, being able to dress unaided, learning to swim, or packing bags for school or for a sleepover can be openly appreciated.

- Appreciation energizes. When children hear your appreciation they feel able to move forward. Those who receive little can get emotionally and developmentally stuck and become demoralized.

- Many schools have reward systems that acknowledge achievement for each individual rather than what is exceptional for the group.

- Appreciate a wide variety of skills and knowledge, not simply those related to academic learning, on which most lessons concentrate.

Approve of who he is

Approval is the green light to grow, to carry on in the same way because he is good and fine as he is. Boys need this not only from their mothers, but also from their fathers, if this is practical or possible, or, if not, from an alternative father figure. As soon as boys start to identify more closely with being male, usually around the age of eight, they benefit from having an adult male available not just to approve of them but also to act as a positive role model as they explore ideas of masculinity and what it might mean for them. Male friends, uncles or cousins, or a friendly neighbor may be able to step in when a father is absent. At the very least, mothers should be careful never to disparage men within a boy's earshot, and they can help by speaking favorably of men in general or particular whenever possible.

But gender is only one aspect of a boy's identity—one of the later spoonfuls of color added to his personality palette. He is already an individual, and he needs to feel approved of for all his strengths, weaknesses, fears, habits, and eccentricities.

Parents	Teachers
• Hear his side of the story. Assume the best of him, not the worst.	• Avoid stereotyping. Each boy is an individual, not a replica of anyone, even an older sibling.
• Let him tell you about his disappointments, and realize what they mean to him.	• Acknowledge that each student's point of view is the result of his unique experiences over the years.
• Respect his ideas (of what to play or wear), his methods (of how to study), and his preferences when these are important.	• Accept that different children learn in different ways, and be tolerant of each one's preferred style.
• Listen to what he has to say, keeping your opinions to yourself unless he asks for them.	

4 | Admire rather than adore

When parents put their son on a pedestal, they present him with a very hard act to follow. Most boys would prefer not to have that pressure. The following conversation between a mother and her four-year-old son highlights the problem: "I adore you, Jamie!" "Don't adore me, Mommy." "Why not?" "Because I cry too much."

What Jamie was trying to say was "It is too much for me always to behave in a way that pleases you and makes you adore me. I know I'm not that good all the time, because I cry a lot, which makes you mad, and I can tell that you don't adore me then."

Adoration is a form of worship, and children don't want to be treated as a god. We may feel it privately, for most of us think our children are heavenly, but we should express something more measured. We can admire how any boy in our care copes in a particular situation, admire how he manages to overcome his fears, or admire how he approaches a problem. He will realize he is in command during these moments, and the occasion is specific. What he certainly cannot directly control are our feelings: These are our business, and it is unfair to load him with any responsibility for these. Even when he cries, we should show we love him for being who he is.

Parents	Teachers

- Don't put him on a pedestal. Let him feel special to you because he is yours, but let him feel normal in relation to his peers.

- Show admiration for what he does—"Well done!" "Nice work!" "Great score!"—but don't worship the ground he walks on.

- Keep him free of emotional obligations to you: Don't require him to earn your love or behave so as to keep you entranced.

- Teachers are unlikely to "adore" a particular child in their class, but having one or two favorites is quite common. Boys in general feel uncomfortable being favored—it singles them out when they'd prefer to be one of the boys.

- Try to keep your admiration in proportion, and always keep it private. Public accolades for creditable work can lead to teasing about being teacher's pet. Instead, have a quick word as he leaves the classroom, or if you use e-mail in school, send a brief message.

5 | Attention is what all boys really want

I hate it when adults ignore me! It makes me feel like an ant.

—Tom, age 10

Children need to be noticed. They are very small creatures in a very big world, which is sure to appear huge, confusing, and even intimidating to them. Our supportive attention fires them up; it gives them the energy and confidence to find their way. Without it, they can feel lost and small and insignificant.

Boys also need our appreciative attention. When boys are young, they are learning at a speed that would exhaust most adults. What gives them special pleasure is to gain greater control of their bodies and their life as they become taller, stronger, and better coordinated. They can acquire an enormous sense of pride in their achievements as they reach the top of the jungle gym, learn to jump into the deep end of the swimming pool, manage stunts on their bikes, or simply become sufficiently tall to open the freezer or reach the faucet or light switch. At these moments of personal triumph, their whole self shouts, "Look at me!" If we are absent in either body or mind, they could become dejected and crestfallen.

Parents	Teachers

- Remember that attention seeking is usually attention needing. Give your son more attention if he starts to pester and irritate you, but only after he has calmed down.

- When you are focusing on him, give him your full attention: Don't answer the telephone; don't sneak in a coffee with a friend on your special trip out together; and refer to any special chats or episodes later, so he knows you were paying attention.

- Think of the everyday things you do that he might feel excluded from and the ways he could become more involved. For example, could you show him your workplace?

- Identify the boys you have contact with who are quiet or withdrawn. Speak briefly to each one around school several times over the next few weeks.

- If a quiet boy is with friends when you think to reach out to him, ask if he has a moment to discuss something, and include a practical issue as well as something affirming so that he can provide a safe answer to his friends if they ask what you wanted.

- Just a smile and a "How're things?" could be enough.

6 | Anticipate a boy's problems and feelings

Boys, more than girls, live in the here and now. They act and react quickly and want to get things done and over with and then move on. Most boys are less inclined than girls to think ahead to the possible consequences of their actions and are therefore more likely to find themselves in trouble. Boys also tend to blank out thoughts about things they'd prefer weren't happening (or wish did not have to happen), such as cleaning their rooms or packing for a vacation, and rely instead on their belief that they will deal with it when they have to. But boys need to become more mindful of the future—delightful though their energetic, youthful spontaneity is—because they need to learn to plan, anticipate, be careful and caring, and take responsibility.

Demonstrate by example and try to anticipate how a boy may respond to something potentially difficult that is coming up in order to help him prepare. Encourage him to be honest about and reflect on his feelings by chatting about how you felt when it happened to you, or say, "I imagine that was/could be difficult for you." Although we would not want to generate anxiety where none exists, boys can be relieved to discover someone understands any, often heavily disguised, worry.

Parents	Teachers

- Anticipate how your son might react to something that is about to happen. If he will be distressed or disappointed, tell him you realize that, and address the details that may worry him to put him more at ease. He will at least feel accepted and understood.

- Through positive feedback and prompting, and through lots of talk that focuses on today's, yesterday's, and tomorrow's events, we can help him to anticipate outcomes and to become more sensitive to other people's likely reactions.

- Rather than allow him to stay locked safely in the present, help him to reflect on the past and the future. Help him to make sense of these if they are uncomfortable.

- Try to imagine the particular difficulty a boy who is struggling might confront with a particular assignment. Approach him and acknowledge this, perhaps suggesting a few helpful guidelines.

- Give him faith in his ability to do the assignment well enough, in a way that represents a learning advance for him.

7 Help a boy achieve his aims

My ten-year-old son decided he wanted to undertake a detailed nature survey of the local parkland. He was passionate about small creatures and wanted to lay small mammal traps to do a count, as well as search for beetles and other insects. I took him to the nearest specialist map shop and bought a large-scale map of the area. Then I helped him to draw lines on it to divide it into smaller squares. He started to dig around and record his findings but couldn't keep it up. It was too big a project. But at least he realized that I respected his dreams and that he could make something happen.

Boys can have short attention spans and can lose heart and direction easily. Although they may resent interference, they generally appreciate receiving help to stay on track when a task becomes tedious or to bring any fanciful ideas to fruition when their imagination takes off. Without getting pushy or demanding, adults can help boys achieve their dreams. We can shore up their faith in themselves and teach them how to translate often elaborate ideas into practical action.

Parents	Teachers

- Whereas it may be pushy to ensure that a boy reaches the goals we determine, it is wholly supportive and encouraging when we help him identify practical pathways to reach those goals he sets for himself.

- Help your son to set out a detailed plan that will enable him to achieve his more challenging aspirations.

- Ask him what equipment or help he needs, but don't take over and make it your project.

- It is important that children receive constructive feedback that helps them to develop their understanding and, through this process, learn how to increasingly manage their own progress.

- Boys will be helped to achieve their aims when they are actively involved in planning their work and carrying out their plan. End with a review of what went right and wrong in order to assess how to approach that same task next time. This is known as *feedback for learning;* in shorthand, plan, do, review, then reframe.

8 | Acknowledge his personal strengths

Boys don't have to be "good at" something before they gain our attention and regard. Each possesses personal qualities, inclinations, interests, and strengths that can be noted, appreciated, and—most important—brought to his attention. Praise should always encompass far more than pats on the back for specific accomplishments. If we reflect back and give a name to some of the warmer, caring qualities he demonstrates to his brothers and sisters, to us, or to his friends, as well as to those strengths, such as perseverance and determination, that encourage achievement, he will be able to develop a picture of his whole self just as he can see his physical self in a mirror. This type of praise will help him to become more aware of his social qualities and to recognize that these are important, too.

The kinds of personal strengths we can acknowledge and name include the following: thoughtfulness, understanding, being good at sharing, caring, being forthright, curiosity, a sense of humor, a good memory, being well-organized, imagination, ability to relax, being carefree, good powers of concentration, interest in ideas, and being well coordinated, to name several.

Parents	Teachers
• Acknowledge your son's full range of possible talents and interests.	• Acknowledge that each child is an individual with a right to be heard and respected.
• Acknowledge his positive thoughts as well as his positive deeds.	• List the personal strengths of any boy whose behavior is causing concern, and make sure he and other children realize you appreciate these.
• Focus on the necessary "doing" aspects of achievement—the inclination to try—as well as the degree to which he tried by the end of the process.	• Choose him to perform any task that might use or develop his personal strengths.
	• Take care to balance out your attention sufficiently so an attempt to help one individual does not come across as favoritism.

9 | Be aware and alert

We cannot talk about what we have noticed in a boy unless we remain aware of his moods, what has delighted him, his preferences, and so on. We can be with our child all day without really noticing any of these, or we can see our son for only two or three hours a day and be acutely sensitive to his body language, expressions, tone of voice, choices, and demeanor.

Being aware does not necessarily mean we should discuss every concern or interpretation then and there, but we would be wise to note it and watch for a possible pattern. For boys especially, too much expressed "sensitivity" can feel intrusive. "Stop trying to get inside my head!" was one eleven-year-old's frustrated cry to his mother when she was trying hard to be empathic. Especially after a tiring day at school, most boys want to relax, remain quiet, and reflect. Any rebuff, often indicated by a curt "Fine," is not necessarily a sign of big trouble he'd rather keep private, just the need to be quiet and alone.

Parents	Teachers

- Watch to see how he relates to his brothers and sisters. Compliment him if he is helpful, kind, and caring or if he ignores being baited by others.

- Make a mental note of which events excite him and which tend to make him sad or disappointed.

- Be careful not to seem like a spy: "I have generally noticed/been aware/it's become clear to me that . . . " is better than "I have been watching you from a distance and I've seen you be really . . . "

- If something important is to happen at school— a test, a notable visitor, a special fun class, a class play—remember to ask how it went.

- It is easy to comment positively on students' work when they hand it in as an assignment but less easy to remark on their wider attitudes and supportive behavior unless you look out for these.

- Be alert for signs of sadness or depression. Sensitivity to these will imply you have bothered to notice and know him well enough to realize things aren't quite right.

10 | His, not your, aspirations matter most

I wanted to major in economics and politics at college, but my parents were ambitious for me and had set their hearts on my becoming a doctor. They paid the fees so I felt I had no choice. I eventually became a psychiatrist and have taken up some important social and political issues, but I haven't quite forgiven them.

—James, age 32

Many parents are keen to give their sons a better life. The parents above, who were recent immigrants, thought that giving their son clear aspirations for a stable and successful professional future would be the best thing that they could do for him. It is certainly better that we look hopefully on his future prospects than that we profess doubt and derision, but it is potentially dangerous to be as predetermined as these parents were.

This degree of direction may, for example, lead a parent to stifle some special interest for fear it could divert a son from the chosen path. Or a parent's dreams may become obvious, and he may thwart them out of spite. He may, though, enjoy following this destiny and see it as a gently amusing game. The most valuable thing we can nurture in our sons is the confidence, optimism, trust, motivation, space, and self-determination to develop their own aspirations with a commitment that should give us pleasure.

Parents	Teachers
• Offer plenty of attention, affirmation, and structure so your son has the confidence to imagine himself doing well and the creativity to aspire.	• Learning should help us all to explore "our possible selves." It should open up possibilities, not close them down.
• Help to ground those aspirations in reality by discussing practical plans for making them happen.	• Help boys to express their aspirations. After a good piece of work or a good class, ask where a boy sees this leading or what he has in mind for his future because you see a bright future for him.
• Even small boys express wishes and desires: "I want to draw a plan of the backyard"; "I'd like to play a Star Wars® game when Sam comes over"; "I'd like to play guitar." If you help to make these happen, he will know it is safe to dream and possible to influence his own destiny.	• From a young age, boys can be encouraged to consider the future and imagine where they see themselves, in terms of jobs, family situation, and pastimes, and where they might live. Any fanciful answers can be prompted with "That's great! Now your task is to plan how you can make this happen."
• Help to make his future feel safe and full of potential by creating a secure present.	

Chapter 3

The Basic Principles of Effective Praise

Keeping praise effective is important. There is no point in praising a boy if he is going to end up feeling oppressed or manipulated by our praise or resentful because we have not got it right. Resentful children have a tendency to hit back where it hurts most. If we show that his performance on the soccer or baseball field, in school, or on the stage is the part of him that really matters to us, he might decide to forgo any of these activities just to pay us back for our interference or to deflect the constant pressure.

We praise children because we believe it helps them, so there is no point in trying to build a child's confidence if it leads to the opposite: a child with an uncertain sense of self-worth who needs constant reinforcement and continuous success to remain convinced of his ability and our approval. It is not to any child's advantage to become so used to praise that its absence implies disapproval or disappointment.

The hallmarks of constructive praise include the following:

Strengthen self-belief. Generalize the achievement and pay as much attention to a boy's capacity to achieve as to the specific outcome. Possible comments are "You're good at *that sort of thing*" or "Now that you've done it once, you should have the confidence to understand it next time and in the future."

Leave him with the possibility and opportunity to change. Allow him to be different or to do something differently next time. Praise should not lock any boy into a single way to please, perform, or do things by being too narrow and focused. Children develop and change as they mature and grow, as adults do, which is one of the potential delights of living for all of us.

Deter dependence. Encourage him gradually to judge things for himself, and make clear your confidence in his ability to do so. This will also help him to realize that what matters most is the pattern of his personal progress and learning, not the precise outcome on any specific occasion.

It may seem hard to offer enough praise to encourage a child yet avoid the danger of overdoing it, but it is not so difficult if the ten basic principles of constructive praise, set out in the next ten tips, are followed.

11 | Let him impress you

Boys love it when someone they respect and admire is clearly, freely, and genuinely impressed by something they have done. Showing and stating you are impressed is a very effective and straightforward form of praise, which helps boys to stand taller, inspired by extra confidence and pleasure.

Being impressed sidesteps the judgment that is implied in so much praise. Most important, it is unconditional. "I am really impressed!" or "That was impressive!" says it all—no "ifs" and "buts" to qualify or detract from the message. There is nothing grudging about being impressed, and when boys hear it they are able to feel top dog.

Fathers who are able to be impressed by their sons clear the air of competition. They level the playing field, for they show they don't need to prove that they're stronger, better, or more clever. And being impressed doesn't mean a boy has "won" in some way or will stop trying. It simply signifies respect and admiration, which is what boys thirst for.

Parents	Teachers
• Compare your son favorably with you as a child: "I couldn't have managed that when I was your age," "I wish I'd been able to do/draw/ sing as well as you can."	• "You showed an impressive degree of understanding in that essay."
• "I thought you played impressively well. Were you pleased with what you did?"	• "I'm impressed that this piece of work is so much better laid out. It must have taken you longer, but thanks for giving it extra time."
• When playing any game, let a little one win in little ways, and show you're impressed by his increasing skill.	• "That's an impressive improvement."
• Ask him to help you fix things, organize things, decide things, clean things; then say, "Wow, you're an ace at that, aren't you?"	• Give boys responsibilities, such as reporting back on group discussions and looking up information for everyone's benefit. Show how impressed you are by his competence.

12 | Make it mean something—be specific

It helps boys to feel comfortable about accepting praise if it is descriptive and specific, that is, related to a particular piece of work, achievement, or action and to a particular aspect of it. Of course, describing something in detail proves without doubt that you have noticed your son's effort or thoughtfulness, but your observations also help the feedback to be accurate and relevant while having the additional advantage of avoiding being judgmental.

Boys, though, benefit particularly from hearing detail about both achievements and mistakes. Some boys' overconfidence can predispose them to deny that they need to know anything. They're more likely to claim they did well because they're "good" at something, than because they practiced in a particular way, developed good memory techniques, or finally understood something. Similarly, they're inclined to claim they did badly because they did not train or revise properly, because the test or competition was stupid, or the teacher was inept. Offering detail will help to convince your son he can be confident about his future performances because he understands what it is he's doing right and can repeat it. Self-satisfaction and arrogance may sometimes get a boy out of a hard place, but they don't help anyone who needs to make solid progress step by step.

Parents	Teachers

Parents

- Describe in some detail what your son has done that is pleasing so he's clear about what's right in his approach and what he needs to repeat next time.

- When reviewing his artwork, discuss the colors used or the size or shape. Ask why or whether he likes what he's done, whether he planned it, or if it just turned out that way.

- Describe what you appreciated about how he behaved after the event rather than comment every few minutes as the occasion unfolds.

Teachers

- Encourage boys to evaluate each other's work after the class has discussed important points to watch out for.

- Boys need to know in detail what they did right and wrong, so comments and marks should be full and clear at the same time as encouraging.

- Help a boy to feel it is okay to be proud of good work: "I bet you felt pretty happy with this piece of work. You should."

13 Keep praise private

I don't mind a teacher saying something like "Well done" or "I liked this" when he hands back work in class, but it totally freaks you out if he goes on and on about how good it was. It's so embarrassing!

—Nathan, age 13

I like it when it's given as part of the team effort—you know, "The baseball team did well in their league game, and Gerry Thomas got four of the five home runs," but if it was "Gerry Thomas was the star of the game; he held it all together," that's not so good.

—Gerry, age 16

As boys grow older, and especially when they get to high school or college, praise given in public, even in front of the class, tends to make them squirm. They are not sure how to react to praise in front of classmates because it is probably not acceptable to admit to and show they are pleased, and they do not want anyone to think that they've worked hard enough to get the attention of the teacher, who may not be liked by everyone.

It's easier to give praise at home, but even then, everyday praise should be a private matter between parent and son, not paraded as something for siblings to become jealous of.

| Parents | Teachers |

- Celebration is a public statement, but everyday praise should be private.

- Ask yourself whose business this is. Usually, it relates only to parent and child, for it is no one else's responsibility.

- Keeping praise private helps to keep it in proportion. The more people you tell, or the more people who are present when you praise your son, the more it will seem to grow in importance and court unintended consequences.

- Private praise helps to focus a boy safely on his personal progress. Public praise may encourage unhelpful competition and may lead boys to work for the wrong reasons.

- Don't assume all boys want public recognition in, for example, an assembly. Some may underperform to avoid being accused of being a teacher's pet.

- Send parents a note detailing a boy's improvement. Most boys would prefer parents to know rather than classmates.

- Have a quiet word with a student as he leaves the class if you want to say a special "Well done."

14 Let the boy take all the credit

It is often taken as a sign of good teaching or parenting if a child excels, so an adult may seek to claim credit when a student, son, or class does well. Of course, we might have had some influence, by reading to him a great deal when he was young, driving him to and from extra classes or training, helping him with his math, encouraging him to keep a daily diary, or nurturing any special fascination with things like insects, electronics, or dinosaurs that might have livened his mind. But his actual achievement—on the day—is always his, and it is selfish and shortsighted to suggest anything else. If we need to boost our own self-esteem through claiming success on the back of our child's, the most obvious message is that success is something he, too, needs before he can feel acceptable and complete.

In the same vein, if we help in a manner that makes him believe that his success was due to us, not him, it dilutes the potential gain in his self-belief and confidence, which would be a great pity if he could have achieved it on his own.

Parents	Teachers

Parents

- Never attribute any of your son's success to you. Make it clear that he can feel 100 percent it was his work; otherwise, he may feel he needs you next time, too.

- If you find yourself saying, "That homework we did . . . what was our mark?" realize that you could be about to walk off not only with some of the credit but also with ownership of the work!

- If he mentions your help, make it clear that it was he who delivered on the day, and that further help from you won't be necessary.

Teachers

- In the context of standardized tests, it is hard not to claim much of the credit if a whole class does better than expected. Nevertheless, each child must feel he did it himself, even if he was well taught by you!

- The more detail a boy has about why he did well, the more he can see and believe it was his knowledge, learning, and application that took him there.

15 | Be careful with judgment

My friend was very keen on manners. Her little boy had to be polite and aware of others at all times, even though he was only five or six. He was praised well for this. But if he bumped into someone while walking down the street, dropped a candy wrapper, or didn't think to step aside for a stroller, he was reprimanded for his disappointing behavior. He couldn't cope with being judged for things he was too young to control, and at home he regressed, ending up wanting to feed from a bottle again like a baby.

Children need to be noticed rather than judged. It is fine to evaluate some of what they do, but it is not fine to be judgmental about who they are. When children are young, they cannot conceptualize this distinction. They don't want to be monitored and evaluated from dawn to dusk, bearing the burden of always being watched and having to stay in line. Expectations must always be appropriate and evaluative praise reserved for actions that boys can easily change. Children thrive when they are open and feel free within safe limits, not when they are constantly having to look over their shoulder, waiting for good or bad comments.

Parents	Teachers

- Make sure your expectations are age-appropriate. Boisterous boys may be enthusiastic rather than thoughtless, careless, or determinedly naughty.

- Keep shame and guilt out of it. Your son will feel these naturally if he believes he has let himself down, but don't set out to make him feel ashamed and guilty just because you feel disappointed.

- You bring about what you fear. Many boys will flaunt bad behavior if they expect to be reprimanded. It ends the waiting and puts them in control, so it's less humiliating.

- Encourage boys to assess their own work.

- Keep feedback neutral and descriptive rather than either flattering or harsh and negative.

- Shame often encourages boys to ignore or reject suggestions for improvement. Use it very sparingly, if at all.

Be truthful, not gushing

Boys don't feel comfortable with what they might view as "gush and mush"—overenthusiastic adulation that seems unrelated to the effort entailed and is certainly not expected, let alone desired. It is too emotional and too intimate and encourages them to believe that they are responsible for a parent's excessive delight and that it's your delight that counts. What counts, of course, is their own sense of pride, fulfillment, and pleasure—they must eventually do things to a standard to please themselves, not to gain riotous applause from the parental gallery.

False praise is not only offensive and insulting; it also does not help boys to develop good judgment. Over time, they must learn to judge their effort and work for themselves. If we go overboard when they know something could have been done better, they will find it harder to tell what is good enough and what could be improved upon. Boys tend naturally to overvalue their work. Gushing adds to that unhelpful tendency.

Parents	Teachers

- Don't pretend, but be positive and upbeat when you can. Make the scope for improvement very clear, and encourage your son to accept and understand his shortcomings: "I don't quite call this a clean room. You've done well so far, but that pile of comics still needs to be sorted. When you've finished, I'll bring you up a treat and admire the room!"

- Point to the pleasure he gets, so he learns to perform for his gain, not yours.

- Some boys need more of a boost and find measured praise hard to believe. However, these boys just need praise said more often, not more enthusiastically or exaggeratedly, because they won't believe that either.

- If you are honest but encouraging about the bad, students will be more inclined to believe honestly given praise.

17 | Praise the process, not the product

Many skeptics of the value of praise complain that the quality of the product does matter—and more than the process. What is the point, they argue, in claiming something is good when it is not, and in ignoring the reason—that someone simply did not try hard enough when he could obviously do better?

Naturally, at some point the quality does matter, and boys should, indeed, be called to account for behavior or performance that suggests they didn't apply themselves, but this position misunderstands the advice. Trying is always valuable—no one makes any progress without some commitment and effort applied to learning more or doing better. Effort, at the beginning, is necessarily often crude and inefficient, but that is the route we all took—and we have survived! In addition, what younger boys produce is always flawed compared with what we could do, and they cannot continuously be told something is not good enough. Effort involves process, or "doing," skills such as determination and tenacity, which need to be valued and encouraged.

Parents	Teachers
• Remember that "process" includes interest, application, determination, and good work habits, and that these attributes should be valued as part of learning and growing.	• Through use of the "plan, do, review" model of learning (see Tip 7), children can begin to reflect on their working style and learn to judge the effectiveness of their efforts.
• Take seriously any effort mark supplied by your son's school. Sensitive to his age and stage, schools often judge effort better than parents.	
• Young children don't understand what it means to try hard or concentrate. Encourage this by reading through longer stories or playing board games that take time, patience, and thought.	
• Learning is an emotional process, so ask if it was hard, if he worried about the outcome, or if he faltered in the middle.	

For best effect, praise should be given straight, with no "ifs" and "buts," no sarcasm, no reminders of past failures or other putdowns to dilute its effect.

And it should be given right away whenever possible, as that conveys spontaneity. Sometimes the positive response does not occur to us at the time, or we are busy with other children so don't really take in the relevant information. A parent who is out of town for work should be primed to say something appreciative on the telephone that day rather than wait until the homecoming and receive the lists of good deeds that need complimenting. Since many boys are embarrassed by overt and public praise, they would rather hear an informal, more natural comment at the time (even if that means it is less well informed) than a measured, serious assessment delivered later.

Better late than never is certainly advisable, but even better to say it sooner rather than later, provided you do not do it so often that you provide an irritating and counterproductive running commentary.

Parents	Teachers
• Children take praise very seriously, so treat it seriously. As it's not the moment for jokes, don't be sarcastic if you want your comments to be effective.	• The quicker you can give feedback on work done, the more a boy will learn from your comments because he will still remember how he approached the task.
• If you didn't respond at the time, make amends by saying something like "I thought again about what you told me, properly this time. Sounds like you did really well and it was important. That's terrific."	• If you make positive comments on children's personalities, interests, sociability, and style, these can be given right away.
• Say it as if you mean it, and while you are looking at your child, not as you turn to leave the room.	

19 Focus on the achievement, rather than on the boy

"Focus on the behavior, not the child" is recommended by most parenting pundits. It is fundamental and is as relevant when praising a boy as it is when reprimanding or disciplining him. Separating children from their behavior makes a great deal of sense in relation to discipline. Letting a child know he's loved—that we're just not wild about what he's done—allows every child to hold onto that all-important sense of self-worth that feeds self-respect and the will to do well.

In relation to praise, we should always focus on what it is our son has achieved, not on who he is. "That was terrific, what you managed to do' is a far less emotionally entangling thing to say than "You're so wonderful to have got that far/done that. I love you so much!" He may not feel so wonderful, knowing full well he didn't pull out all the stops for this event. He may realize, too, that you scold him when he has been naughty, so he knows he is not always so wonderful. We should love and feel proud of our boys all the time and not ration these feelings, reserving them for when they do well.

Parents	Teachers

- Boys under three cannot separate what they do from who they are, so very young boys need praise kept very simple. Approval words that mention the achievement will be enough, such as "Well tried!" "Eating all your dinner was great"; "Great catch!" "Lovely picture"; "Nice job waiting your turn."

- From about age ten, boys begin to feel more emotionally independent. They no longer want public displays of affection because they are trying to be free. Surprise hugs are great, but praise should always commend the achievement, not your son. "That was a clever thing to do," not "You are so clever."

- Boys may like to feel liked, as in accepted and enjoyed, by their teachers, but they tend not to relish favoritism or personal comments. "John always gives his work in on time" is easier to accept than "John's the only reliable boy here when it comes to handing in work."

- Say, "That exercise you did for me last month was great. That shows you can do it," rather than "You're a clever boy, if only you'd believe it. Of course you'll do it fine."

20 | Ask him how he wants praise delivered

After football on a Saturday my twelve-year-old son often asks me how I thought he played, and I reply, "How do you want it?" We have this scheme: He can ask for it "straight," "gentle," or "I'll guess what you think." If he's feeling up to an honest account that he guesses ought to be critical, he'll say, "straight."

There are two parties in any learning situation—the teller and the person being told. To be effective as a mentor, coach, or mere supporter, we have to understand how the information we offer could be received. Truth and honesty may be what we're ready to give, but if the boy who receives the "telling" isn't ready to hear that, he can block it out by denying or ignoring it.

So if we decide the time has come not to beat around the bush anymore, either because he's now older and may not need so much coddling or because he has started to misjudge himself, we can begin by giving him some control over the level of honesty in any feedback. If we give him the choice of hearing the good news or the bad news first, he's far more likely to remain receptive to the entire message.

Parents	Teachers

- Be sensitive to the moment: Consider the context and recent events. If he's had a tough time and disappointments elsewhere, don't choose that moment to "give it to him straight"!

- If you have not put the question back to him and asked him what he thinks, begin your reply, *"I think you know this already* . . . you were a bit slow off the mark at the start/you weren't responding quickly enough." The point is to encourage him to have faith in his own assessment, not to become dependent on you.

- Always ask at the end, "Did you think my comment was fair?"

- Check afterward how your comment was received: "I was quite honest with you on that. Did it upset you, or was it helpful?"

- Feedback is a process, and learning is a two-way street. Allow and encourage students to reflect and discuss with you how they react to your style and approach. Listen to class opinions but note individual views, too.

Chapter 4

Ages and Stages: Adapting to Development

The five separate stages of childhood mark out key changes in children's needs, in what they are progressively able to do, how they are able to think, what they are able to understand, and therefore how they see themselves. It is clear, then, that parents and teachers need to be sensitive to these changes and adjust their praise style and strategies as boys mature.

Newborn babies are engrossed with their physical needs and very dependent for these on their carer. But they also respond vigorously to close attention and react to it very physically—every bit of their body moves and their whole being seems engaged in the communication. Some research has indicated that baby boys are particularly active: They move more than girls inside the womb and are more energetic after they are born.

Newborn babies have to face a bewildering array of sounds, smells, signs, and behaviors. The challenge for carers is to make them feel physically and emotionally safe by establishing reliable close contact and familiarity through regular routines and patterns.

Sometime during the second year, the baby becomes a walking and talking toddler. These skills make him feel far more independent, and his sense of self becomes clearly established. He wants to explore, experiment, and examine everything. Though he's now capable of doing so much more, the overwhelming experience for a boy can be one of failure and incompetence as he stumbles and fumbles, breaks things, misjudges things, and tries to make sense of all the rules that suddenly appear.

At this age, boys are generally less well coordinated than girls, far clumsier, and less able to explain themselves. What a toddler needs from parents and carers keen to nurture his self-esteem is a great deal of tolerance of the genuine and inevitable mistakes made during the steepest learning curve of his life. Plenty of encouragement for each small step made toward self-management and self-control, tolerance of his frustrations, and lots of attention will help him to feel noticed, competent, understood, and affirmed.

From the age of four to about seven, boys see life very simply: Things are either good or bad, right or wrong, which also means that they see themselves in the same simple terms, as either a good boy or a bad boy. Subtlety is not what they're about or what they see, so parents should think carefully about the balance of positive and negative feedback they give. Most of the time these school-aged children want to please, provided they're not angry about feeling left out or being unloved. They still rely on copying—parents, brothers, sisters, and increasingly friends—for a lot of their learning, and they need signs of approval that they're on the right track.

In the preteen, or "tween," years, boys may become more suspicious of parents' use of praise or simply get bored with trying to please: They would prefer to get on with life and not be on constant watch for an adult's approval or disapproval. Tweens are starting to separate, especially from their mothers; are enjoying their growing freedom; and are paying increasing attention to the views of friends. However, they need lots of positive backup as they try out a broader range of skills and activities that their stronger bodies now allow. They invest a huge amount in physical and sporting prowess, so any emerging competence in ball skills, blading, bike stunts, or skateboarding can be noticed and remarked upon. Smaller boys who are later developers may need extra help to feel proud of talents that are less dependent on strength. In other words, at this stage, appreciation of what they can now do is at least as important as approval of who they are. Sibling rivalry could begin to focus on competing talents, so make sure all children feel equally loved and accepted despite their varying abilities and talents.

Teenage boys still like to be praised, but if praise goes over the top they feel uncomfortable. They enjoy their efforts being noticed and appreciated, but they are beginning to judge much more for themselves and know exactly how big a deal any achievement is. As one fifteen-year-old boy said, "My father doesn't praise me as much, so when it comes from him, I get more of a rush, and I feel good. It feels like it's really worthwhile." But another said, "As you get older you don't expect praise so much. You're more independent. It gets more patronizing when it's too frequent."

One issue with teenage boys is that their increasing independence makes it harder to know what they're doing, good or bad. Any inquisition is likely to feel intrusive and make them retreat. Their very need for more privacy suggests they want parents less and more time alone to work things out for themselves. So lie low, save your celebrations for the notable successes, and in the meantime, focus on affirmation. Make sure, too, that, far from criticizing their views and values, their friends, ideas, clothes, passions, or creativity, you actively respect their right to express themselves and be different from you. These expressions are essential elements of their maturing self-confidence and identity.

21 Make babies feel safe and secure

Babies are able to read people long before they can read words. They notice and recognize our moods, tone of voice, and physical movements long before they can understand what is being said. They will be more sensitive to these modes of communication than possibly at any other time of their lives, as it is by recognizing patterns in these that they feel linked to our world. Almost from the moment of birth we know that babies copy as a way to communicate because they can poke out the tip of their tongue when someone does it to them at close range. They let us know how they feel through their limbs, which either flail in distress or twitch excitedly, and, of course, through crying and smiling. Their cries may express hunger, discomfort, loneliness, boredom, or anxiety—any of which an adult might feel. By meeting their need for food, safety, love, warmth, and security, we demonstrate that we understand them and their need for us, which is sufficiently affirming to them so that we can call it praise. What matters to them is less *what* we say than that we say, or even sing, something to them in tones that are familiar and sound soothing. Simply talking, even out of view, tells them that we are near. Paying closer attention and playing with their toes and fingers shows more directly that we care and signifies that they can rely on us.

Parents	Teachers

- At this age, attention seeking is definitely attention needing. Babies become obviously distressed when someone who is playing with them looks or moves away, and they come alive when we connect with them directly.

- Choose a song, or make one up, to sing at each clear stage of their day: to mark feeding, bath time, diaper changing, or going to collect an older sibling, for example. Your boy will then begin to recognize the tunes and become familiar with the day's regular routines.

- Physical closeness— holding and carrying him, playing with his nose or chin, fingers, and toes—establishes and helps him to experience his physical boundaries and thus gives him his first sense of self.

- One-to-one contact with young babies is very important to ground their sense of being, safety and significance.

- Regular social, visual, and emotional contact and stimulation helps their newly formed brains to establish positive neural connections.

- Routines are vital to give any baby or young child a sense of safety, order, and security.

Babies must feel they're important

As far as anyone can tell, new babies have very little awareness of having a separate identity: They merge with their caregiver as one. One key way in which they begin to realize that they matter to us and develop that sense of being a significant and separate person is to have us be in tune with them and responsive to the signals they send out. Psychologists call this form of give-and-take, notice-and-react style of interacting *synchronicity* and *reciprocity*. It is comforting for babies, even at this level, to know that they can communicate and be heard and understood. This is a far cry from the scheduled, overorganized, packaged-up, and packed-off babies who are required to fit in to other people's superimposed, insensitive, and fixed routines—though it has already been said that they need some routine.

To reciprocate implies respect for the growing person and his developing personality. This requires that we look, listen and notice, respond, and love and care.

Parents	Teachers

- Allow your son to develop his own patterns and pace, and respect these.

- Babies work very hard to form an intimate relationship with their caregiver. If we fail to notice their efforts and ignore them, they will soon stop trying and switch off.

- Playing with his fingers, face, and toes; holding him tight and sharing with him the rhythm of our body, as he shares his with us; and responding to his fears, delights, and sufficiency in relation to food, sleep, or entertainment—all of these allow him to sense our deep love and regard for his being and welfare.

- Endeavor to maintain a carer-infant ratio that enables individual infants' patterns to be respected, within a structure that offers familiarity and security.

- Professional convenience matters, but not if it is acquired at the expense of infant health and contentedness.

23 Give your toddler a positive view of himself

Toddlers have a hard time because they make lots of mistakes and have accidents. They can irritate their parents sometimes beyond measure as they try to carve out space for themselves and strive to be listened to in a family's otherwise busy life. Living with a toddler can be a constant battle, and if it is, it can be well nigh impossible to say enough positive, affirmative, approving, and appreciative things to offset the negative signals we send through shouting, anger, frustration, or simply insisting that our will be done. Yet toddlers, just like older boys, need to feel loved and successful to thrive.

Even during the "terrible twos," a boy will not yet have a clear sense of his unique self. He is as he does. When we reprimand him for what he does, applying the behavior-self rule in order to protect his self-respect, he may still feel personally at fault because he is too young to sense or comprehend the difference.

Physical affirmation—that is, plenty of cuddles and close physical contact—will help him get the simple yet strong message that we continue to love and approve of him despite the hassles.

Parents	Teachers

- Give your son plenty of cuddles and physical reassurance, especially after a "bad patch." Don't necessarily talk, or just say, "That was a tough day!"

- Make a joke to end the arguing: How silly we are, fighting like a cat and a dog!

- Toddlers experience themselves through action. Encourage self-management in as many tasks as possible to help a growing boy feel positive about his role in your world.

- Encourage him to dress himself—even if the socks are odd, the T-shirt back to front, or the colors clashing! Involve him in tasks that don't require perfection, such as digging in the garden or decorating cookies.

- Listening helps boys to feel they matter. Ensure that each boy has someone who will hear his point of view.

- When small children are herded, they feel very insignificant.

- Behavior talks: What is he saying? Get to the bottom of persistent bad behavior quickly, before he becomes sure he is a bad boy.

Until the age of eighteen months, Jack was a model baby. Then, like a typical toddler, he became defiant and disobedient and hated being told no. Jack often flung himself on the floor, kicking and screaming. He would refuse to get out of his car seat and scream if I got his drink wrong or if I tried to get him dressed and ready to go to my mom's. Then I decided to pay him more attention, not to be so strict, to let him decide little things, and to play with him more. The improvement was dramatic.

Toddlers are trying because they're trying it on—almost all the time. Having been carried, sat, fed, dressed, driven, and otherwise "done to" all their short lives, they have recently learned they can be a force to be reckoned with. Toddlers use their expanding vocabulary, stronger bodies, and clearer sense of self and purpose to say no and assert themselves—it's an intoxicating power that they use to get noticed, gain some control, and feel important.

But toddlers also struggle with frustration because they can still do so little for themselves. Their ideas race ahead of their bodies, and they confront real rules. A boy feels more grown up, yet he still can't master every task or express complex and powerful feelings with any subtlety. No wonder it's a tough time for everyone involved!

Parents	Teachers

- Don't take it personally. He does not hate you or want to get at you—he's just expressing feelings he can't put into words.

- Express his frustrations for him: "It must have been hard, being ignored/wanting me to stay with you when I had to leave/being fed up with being told what to do and when to do it, when you felt like staying home and playing."

- Explain to his older brothers and sisters why he feels so mad and why that can make him a nuisance to them.

- Make it clear whenever you can that you know he's not being bad, just finding life hard at the moment.

- Offer chances for boys to play through their frustrations.

- Choose stories to read that represent their difficulties, so they know they're not alone and will feel more understood.

25 Understand what a schoolboy can't understand

Most arguments between parents and children happen when children fail to match up to parental expectations. Older children may choose to play in a rock band rather than follow Mom or Dad into the favored family profession, but clashes with young children usually occur where a child cannot think or behave in the way his parents expect, when he is consequently considered thoughtless, selfish, immature, or even spiteful.

Boys between four and seven or eight are not, and cannot be, grown up. Children develop slowly and in set ways, and boys are often slower developers than girls. "Don't be such a baby!" is especially humiliating when thrown at boys, who will have already picked up that they should be more resilient, reliable, organized, and cooperative and less emotional than they are capable of being. Praise should not be conditional on a boy's understanding more than he can. And criticism should not fly when we are frustrated because he fails to think ahead, understand a complicated rule, anticipate consequences, or imagine how we or anyone else will react. Boys of this age are still very self-oriented: They understand others through assuming that others will feel and act as they do, yet their self-understanding is still very underdeveloped.

Parents	Teachers

- When boys are criticized for falling short, they can easily feel guilty for letting you down and assume there is something wrong with themselves.

- A young boy has to be very grown up and organized at school, so he may want to regress after a trying day and be less responsible at home. Acknowledging this will demonstrate your empathy and understanding.

- Find as many ways as possible to spend and enjoy time with him.

- Whatever he believes you think of him tends to be how he views himself. If he knows you enjoy his company and find him fun, reliable, and capable, he will work and make friends more confidently.

- Young boys can find it harder to fit in and participate in class activities if their home life is stressful. Give any temporary "loner" a special buddy or use paired activities for a while rather than larger group ones.

- Be tolerant of young boys' tendency to fidget. They can often find it difficult to sit still.

- If you feel unsure about the key changes that accompany developmental stages for younger boys, consider taking a course, or find a suitable textbook.

26 | Help a boy to see who he is

Early childhood is when a boy begins to fill out his idea of who he is and what makes him unique. By the time he reaches seven or eight, he will have developed a much clearer sense of what he is good at, what his main likes and dislikes are, what and how he prefers to play, how his parents and other adults react to him, and whether he generally attracts praise or provokes anger or frustration.

Parents can help a boy to clarify and deepen his identity. Instead of simply saying, "I think you're great!" we can be far more specific and say, "You are really great because you are fun to be with, you are very kind to your friends, you love to paint—even though you hate cleaning up afterward—and you clearly prefer to learn by trying things out rather than just accepting what you're told." The more detail we can give, while remaining as nonjudgmental as possible, the better he will understand and appreciate himself.

Parents	Teachers

- Enable your son to feel he belongs to a clear family group and to you. Arrange family outings and events; tell him about his life as a baby and about what your life was like as a child. Involve him in as many of your commitments as is practical or sensible.

- Experiment with the concept of a "personality palette." The more patches of color representing different aspects of his personality, skills, and preferences that you can help him create and place on his personal palette, the more attractive, colorful, and detailed will be the picture he can draw of himself.

- Make sure each child is aware of something—his special passion or a particular skill—that he can feel positive about and proud of. This will help him to have a clear and positive sense of who he is and what he is capable of.

- Help him to be aware of his personal preferences, which will include how he likes to work and his favorite activities and subjects. Talk, too, about the sports teams he supports, if any, his favorite foods, animals, and so on.

27 Encourage your preteen's developing skills

The preteens, or tweens, are renowned as the five years (from eight to twelve) during which children's confidence typically flourishes, provided peer or academic pressures do not undermine it. Tweens' stronger bodies and more capable minds enable them to view things more reflectively, to be more determined to master complex physical and mental tasks, and to work out how to correct mistakes when they get things wrong.

For boys especially, it is their stronger bodies and improved physical coordination during the tween years that give them their greatest sense of pride. They can climb trees better and can kick and hit balls with more skill, and many are beginning to perform all manner of stunts with skate boards and other contraptions. Their skill levels advance by leaps and bounds, and they can become quite assertive and competitive to keep their edge of superiority over classmates and friends. They may also try to lord it over their older or younger siblings.

Feeling more confident about who they are, pre-teen boys love adults to notice their competence and maturing sense of judgment.

Parents	Teachers

- Admire your son's growing competence so he feels proud and capable.

- Give him chances to demonstrate and develop his newly acquired skills. Ask him to help you with practical tasks; then appreciate his contribution.

- Watch him doing something he enjoys, even if it is a computer game you think will be tedious.

- Let him go outside and be active as much as possible, provided you have gone over appropriate safety rules.

- Skills that can be applauded and encouraged include artistic, humor, dramatic, academic, social, communication, sporting, manual dexterity, personal organization, imagination, physical coordination, musical, memory, listening, sound judgment, and empathic skills.

28 Accept your tween's need to act male

My eight-year-old son suddenly developed a whole range of annoying habits, from sniffing outward (without using a tissue), grunting annoyingly, and changing his manner of speaking to generally being rude. I felt I was constantly "on his case." Then someone explained he was almost certainly copying the latest playground style, identifying more with his friends than with his family, and needing to experiment with being a "young man." Of course she was right.

Gender awareness flourishes in the tween years. Boys loosen their emotional ties with their mothers and focus on becoming men. This is the time when boys explore, often clumsily, what it means to be male, slanting their thinking and behavior in ways they consider typical. Tough playground talk often gets brought home.

Preteen boys typically play in large groups to feel more powerful. They can become more assertive with female teachers and their moms. They love to master things that previously frightened them, so they take more risks and get into plenty of mischief.

Parents	**Teachers**

- Try not to criticize your son's new macho attitude continuously. He is a novice trying his new shoes on for size— and they won't fit!

- Teach him what is appropriate. Say this behavior or talk is all right for the playground, but not home.

- As he is trying to separate, maternal praise may be discounted or rejected if it is too gushing. Direct it instead to his achievements and growing competence.

- By understanding why he needs to challenge you, you show that you approve of and accept him.

- Provided he's not in trouble, don't criticize his friends or any close male role model who is helping him into manhood.

- When they flirt with macho attitudes, comment favorably on boys' caring, sharing, and thoughtful qualities, to indicate these human qualities remain important.

- Appreciate pre-teen boys for who they are: their over-confidence often masks a fear of failure.

29 Teenage boys like praise that is measured and moderate

Q: Do you grow out of wanting to be praised?
A: You can't not like it.

—Julio, age 15

Teenage boys still want to hear praise, but they want it to be measured and moderate, not exaggerated or effusive. They are very discriminating by now, and they want you to be honest in your praise. They certainly don't want to be top dog one day and in the dog house the next. Boys this age are becoming far too independent to be swayed by parental reactions, especially when these seem ill informed. What they appreciate most is being noticed and treated as a source of authority about their own welfare, future, and progress. They need to be trusted before they can fully trust their individual ability to evaluate accurately and therefore do well.

Teenage boys value praise and appreciation more when it is sparing. Whether it comes from parents or teachers, boys report that when praise is in plentiful supply, its value decreases.

Parents	Teachers

Parents

- Always ask him how he rates his work, result, or performance before you expound: "That seems like a good outcome/ result, but it's how *you* judge and see it that matters more."

- Ask him if the news is worth passing on: "Do you want to call your dad, or is it not such a big deal?"

- Keep it simple: "Well done!" "That's terrific. Were you pleased?"

- Say something at the end of the week rather than every day.

- Appreciate his views and values more than his daily results so you seem truly interested in and impressed by him rather than obsessed with what he can do.

Teachers

- A teenage boy will enjoy teachers' commendations more readily if these are directed at his hard work and progress rather than at him personally.

- Ensure that any favorable comments are well supported with detail so he knows exactly what it is he has done well and he can believe it.

- For praise to be truly empowering, it must suggest that he has mastered the process just as much as he has mastered the individual task at hand: "You have written a very good essay. You are planning your arguments much better. Your conclusions are more complete, and you are now weighing different approaches. Great."

Help teenage boys to have faith in their future

Gregory was an A student. He did well in high school and went on to do well in college. He thrived on the regular challenges of course work and loved the frequent feedback he got from his largely favorable grades. When he started his first job, though, he seemed to doubt his performance and flounder. He was so used to regular feedback that it took a few months to trust his own judgment and feel at ease.

Self-esteem questionnaires given to boys show that their self-esteem is at its highest at the age of fourteen and then falls gradually to its lowest point at the age of nineteen—the very end of the teens, when they come face to face with their future. Life then becomes deadly serious; it is the moment for big decisions—about college, careers, and commitment. The buck has stopped right there in front of them.

With their son facing such challenges and uncertainty, parents can offer support by commenting favorably on their son's growing maturity and more general competence rather than continuing to highlight the importance of test scores.

Parents	Teachers
• Understand and acknowledge the drop in confidence a teenage boy may experience.	• Encourage teenage boys to look and plan ahead, and commend their positive plans.
• Make him feel he can achieve whatever he sets out to do: "You're clearly capable of getting wherever you decide to go. The future is yours and whatever path you choose, we'll back you."	• Invite previous high school graduates to return to school to describe their personal journeys.
• Show respect for his ideas, plans, views, and values, and assume that others will respect these things, too. Ultimately, they will be more powerful survival tools than his final grades or SATs.	• A mentor can help enormously to boost boys' confidence by focusing them on the possibility of a brighter future than they might otherwise assume.

Chapter 5

What to
Notice and Encourage

It is good practice to find at least three things to notice about our children and comment on positively every day. We should use that comment to point to the past, the present, and the future. We should not be asking *if* a child is good at anything, but instead "What is my child good at?" It is undoubtedly true that there will be something about what he says or does each day for us to notice and appreciate. We just have to be thoughtful and creative.

It is often said that it takes four "praises" to undo the negative impact of one criticism, so how often we should or need to say something encouraging depends in part on how critical we have been. Clearly there needs to be a limit: If we say five hurtful or undermining things to our son in one day, then trying to say twenty positive statements that same day becomes logistically difficult (because we don't necessarily spend that much time together). It can also be very confusing for our son (because we seem to be blowing hot and cold) and can create an atmosphere that is far too intrusive and contrived (because we have to watch so carefully to spot when to pop in the praise). Young boys' attention is apt to wander freely, so they benefit from plentiful positive feedback, delivered frequently and in different ways, to keep them on track. The older boys become, however, the less they need or want wall-to-wall praise, though of course it still gives them a "rush," as one fifteen-year-old put it, when they hear it. Encouragement becomes more necessarily context-bound, focused on a time of particular challenge. Provided we don't lay it on thick, boys will come to value these less frequent endorsements and appreciations of their efforts more highly. Don't forget, though, to continue to say how much you enjoy his company and love who he is. The world ahead of him can seem challenging, even frightening, and he will need every ounce of confidence he can muster.

There is a vast range of possible attributes and achievements to notice in our boys. If we focus on a single area—for example, school grades or work—we have to ask about these things every day to shape what we say. We also need to keep in mind that whichever aspect of his life we comment on could become the part of him he feels we value most and the one he might choose to sabotage if he ever feels sufficiently angry to want to hurt us.

If we pride ourselves on offering a tolerant, warm, and accepting home, we should aim to value, notice, and openly appreciate the following: all aspects of his personality (fears and foibles as well as enthusiasms); skills and talents; general capability; attitudes toward others; and the ability to deal with problems.

31 Appreciate his thinking skills

Boys are typically doers; they are action men. They like to be noisy, active, on the go almost all of the time. This energy is a joy to see and is impressive. It may be exhausting to have to deal with such energy, but most of us would give anything to regain that early vigor—the power to keep going and not stop until we drop, apparently effortlessly. However, the capacity that grows in importance as we mature is the ability to think and reflect. Many boys seem to have a harder time than their sisters reaching that more reflective state. We can help, though, by ensuring that they have quiet thinking time. We can comment positively when they show they have thought something through, and we can encourage the habit of their asking a few more probing questions before they claim they have understood enough.

Boys, of course, think all the time: when they decide what game to play or what clothes to put on in the morning (even if the decision is made in haste!); when they work out how to mend a broken toy, solve an argument with a friend, or suggest a suitable present for a brother or sister. They are forced to reflect when we ask them to explain their behavior. Reflection is an especially useful habit because it encourages them to think ahead. Encourage them to reflect on the past, the present, and the future.

Parents	Teachers

Parents

- Chat with your son about recent events, and ask him to recall what he might have found fun, scary, or difficult: "It's interesting you've mentioned that. Why did you find it scary?"

- Invite him to plan and think ahead when there's free time to fill or there's an unfamiliar situation to face.

- Appreciate his choices: "That's a good idea of what to play!" "I like how you put that sweater and those pants together."

Teachers

- Ask questions such as "Is there anyone here who likes to solve problems?"

- After reading a story, you might say, "I very much liked your ideas about what the character was really thinking in that story."

- Ask boys how they would have liked a story or game to end.

32 Encourage his sociable side

Girls are typically natural talkers; boys are less so. Boys tend to talk later, to read later, to have a more limited vocabulary, and to spend less time in intimate conversation with their friends, a pattern that remains during adolescence and adds further to the verbal gender gap. On top of this, boys' fine motor skills also generally develop later than girls', so they can find writing a slow and often messy business. Words, whether spoken or written, are so often not boys' strong point.

Being more tongue-tied and less adroit at expressing themselves, boys are often more prone to embarrassment and shyness and would prefer to avoid social gatherings. It is typical for a boy to appear momentarily at a family event, then strangely evaporate, or to round up friends and retreat to computer rooms and dens!

However, social skills are valuable, and emotional literacy requires a good vocabulary as well as human understanding. It is important to reward boys when they join in, to welcome their friends, to discourage isolation, and to encourage conversation.

Parents	Teachers
• Value a range of skills that will help your son in social situations, such as helpfulness, understanding, kindness and thoughtfulness, willingness to share, and sorting out or stepping away from arguments. • Expect him to join you sometimes when you visit friends or relatives. • Try to have at least one family meal each week to encourage conversation and friendly banter.	• Most boys prefer to work alone rather than in a group, because they don't have to share or explain, can be competitive, and can do it their way without having to compromise. But group-based tasks encourage sensitivity and sociability. Both ways of working should be included in structured learning. • Groups of both mixed gender and the same gender help boys and girls to appreciate each other's strengths and learn from each other.

Acknowledge that he tried hard

Did you try hard and do your best? That's what matters.

Acknowledging effort is always valuable, for progress is made at every stage on the learning journey. The road there is at least as important as arriving, and each arrival point becomes a staging post from which the learner moves on. It can represent a bigger step forward for someone to realize finally what he's been doing wrong and work out for himself how to correct it than to get something right at the first attempt, but with little awareness of why it was correct.

Effort is important. No one achieves anything significant without it. Effort involves concentration; it means you give it your all. Young children find it hard to concentrate, and they will probably have a poor appreciation of what "trying hard" actually means. But if a young boy's more limited efforts are not respected and valued, it may be harder for him to make the necessary effort when he's older and when the results might matter more.

Parents	Teachers

- Ask your son what he means when he says, "But I tried really hard" before you condemn this statement as a weak excuse.

- Ask for specifics such as how much time was spent on a project; how much time was spent on any diversion such as TV, the computer, or phone calls; whether he took the time to look something up if he wasn't sure; and whether he gave himself time to check over his work.

- If you have every cause to trust him and he said he did his best, not knowing how to do it differently, let it rest at that.

- Do you encourage your students to understand what the terms *effort* and *trying* mean?

- Do you talk about how difficult it can be to persevere, and what students think and feel when they get despondent? Ask anyone who finds a way through when discouraged to describe what he or she docs to achieve this.

34 Notice his organizational skills

Teachers say that when they start secondary school, boys are noticeably less organized and independent than girls, which can interfere with their work. They leave books at home and sports bags on buses, or they forget the deadline for homework. It is a handicap. But the response of most parents or caregivers is to take over and do more things for the boy in their care to prevent disasters. This might make us feel better: We avoid feeling embarrassed when the school complains about our child, and we can see our involvement as caring; but it is not helpful. Boys need to face the consequences of their disorganization, for only then will they make genuine efforts to change their ways.

The good news is that we do not have to wait until things get really bad. There are other options. Well before a child hits rock bottom, we can notice plenty of small examples of organization and self-management and comment favorably on these. Tidying just a corner of a bedroom is progress; returning for an item remembered at the last minute is better than forgetting it until it's too late; and prioritizing commitments on a busy Saturday shows forward thinking.

Parents	Teachers

Parents

- Suggest strategies to aid your son's self-organization, such as making lists, writing reminders on sticky notes, or having a daily to-do list.

- Ask him how he prefers to remember things. It must become his project, not yours, or it may not work.

- Notice when he manages to think and prepare ahead. If it is his way to get everything together at the last minute and it works, that's good enough.

- Better to applaud the developing skills than exude frustration over how far he still has to go. He may be organized in some spheres, just not in the ones you'd like!

Teachers

- A boy's work may look messy in presentation, but if it demonstrates an organized approach, this should be highlighted and commended.

- A focus on metalearning—learning how to learn—will automatically encourage boys to consider how they work.

35 | Value his imagination, however fanciful

I'm a knight. This ruler is my sword, and I'm going to slay the dragon! This little figure is Gandrill— he's lord of the fire and in charge of all these dwarves, who need his fire to make their special daggers that have the power to turn the evil goblins to dust!

—Patrick, age 6

A boy's imagination represents him. It is his own personal creation and not only gives him a sense of freedom but also some productive control over his time. Fantasy allows endless possibilities: He can explore the rare experience of feeling powerful because he can create stories in which he takes a lead role and has unlimited strength. When he is in charge of the story, nothing can go wrong for him unless he wills it, so he can feel totally safe. If we join in on his terms and accept the role he wants us to play, he in effect is in charge of us, too, which will help him to accept our demands much of the rest of the time.

Fantasy encourages mental flexibility and creativity, and both help later with schoolwork. We should appreciate and value his ability to draw, play, and explore imaginatively, and we should occasionally play with him, entering his fantasy.

Parents	Teachers
• Don't devalue any imaginative play. It is part of your son, gives him great skills, and increases his self-knowledge and confidence.	• Fanciful imagination can become distracting, but boys need to be able to be themselves and be encouraged to take risks with possibilities.
• Older boys explore imagination through fantasy. It is not babyish but a healthy counter to the daily grind, provided he can leave it behind when appropriate. Wearing military gear to school, for instance, may be worrisome.	• Boys' imagination sometimes appears in the form of humor or silly pranks. They clown around to get both attention and recognition, but they are also exercising their minds and finding new ways to play with ideas.
• If you join in an imaginative game, don't suddenly talk about the shopping you need to do or what he'd like for a snack. This interruption will shatter his creation and his belief that you take him seriously.	

36 Enjoy his humor

Humor is the spice of life. Around the age of seven or eight, something very important happens to the way children's minds work. They can look at themselves from the outside, can think in abstract categories far more easily, and can play with ideas and see new links. Any parent of a child of this age will tell you that it is at this time parents constantly get asked to laugh at what are usually very bad jokes that their children consider utterly hilarious. Children's joke books tend to be pitched at this age group. Seven- and eight-year-olds often tell jokes picked up from the school yard that they cannot possibly understand, but they find an alternative explanation that makes sense to them. And it's not just the jokes themselves they enjoy; they take great delight in entering that hitherto closed adult world of telling jokes and being in the powerful position of making other people laugh. They become, in effect, the family's very own court jester.

Once we laugh, the show can go on, and on, and on. It gives children huge pleasure to entertain in this way and makes them feel very proud. We must play at being the appreciative audience to our boys and allow them to exercise their new mental muscles and have fun playing with ideas and words.

Parents	Teachers

- Be patient, and try to laugh—or groan—when you are told a joke even if you have heard it plenty of times before.

- Magic tricks are visual jokes that play with the viewer's perceptions and expectations. Encourage any interest in magic, and be tolerant of the performance he may want to give for the family.

- Around the age of ten, boys begin to understand the real humor of jokes and enjoy telling them and making them up. Boys' humor should be valued and given a place in the classroom—though they need to learn when is a good or bad time!

- Linked to this, around the same age a boy may become the class clown, in part because he gains status when he makes others laugh, and in part to avoid answering questions. It might help to defuse an irritating situation by inviting the main "culprit" to prepare a real entertainment session.

Welcome creativity—and
accept the risks and mess involved

Every human being has the capacity to be creative. Young children find it easiest, because they have less idea of what is expected or what is "right" and "wrong." For them, experimentation is fun and helps them to feel in charge and powerful—free from rules and other restrictions. Young boys have not yet absorbed the gender-related social conventions about what boys generally do, so they can all be encouraged to try out a wide range of fun activities, including cooking or painting.

Older boys express their creativity in less organized ways. We should not devalue any activity simply because it seems to lack purpose. Whittling sticks with a penknife, building outdoor camps, mucking around in the mud, and making up rules for a variety of games are all creative pursuits.

Creativity is the expression of originality: It helps children to discover their identity and to experience directly the ways in which they are unique.

Parents	Teachers

- It is not just girls who like to paint. Offer your son plenty of opportunities beyond the classroom to draw, color, paint, and play with modeling clay.

- The majority of celebrity chefs are men, so don't think it is wrong to encourage boys to cook and make up recipes.

- Collage-style pictures can be created from old magazines, from fabrics or dried food, or from twigs, leaves, and petals.

- Boys can become more easily and deeply absorbed in a creative activity if they keep quiet. Try to limit the chat as they explore their ideas and discover what they can create.

- Clearing up afterward helps to instill good organizational habits and encourages a sensible allocation of time. Invite students to gauge how much time is needed.

38 Go deep—endorse his values and beliefs

If one purpose of praise is to make a boy feel good about who he is inside rather than rely on a range of external things, such as clothes, toys, or talents to make him feel comfortable with himself, we need to respect his values and beliefs.

Younger boys will not have developed any consistent system of values for us to appreciate, but they do attach great importance to their friendships and their play. They also possess a natural, passionate concern about fairness that we ignore at our peril. Their beliefs are manifested in the sense that they make of their immediate world: These beliefs form the structure that creates coherence when they face and have to manage confusing events.

From eight or so onward, boys' ability to think in more abstract and conceptual ways and to see things from other people's point of view encourages many to latch onto concerns that focus on others. Whether it is religion, vegetarianism, astronomy, or alternative music, we should endorse their right to develop their own values and interests and respect their beliefs.

Parents	Teachers

- Boys often develop passions that span particular sports, kinds of music, and books involving particular characters. They may also be interested in learning about space and astronomy, cars, or the military. Show interest, and endorse your son's choices and values by helping him to find out more about them.

- If he develops a passion for animals, it means he cares for creatures that need to be looked after. We should respect this tenderness.

- Try to find out about individual students' passions and values, and make reference to these respectfully.

Appreciate his practical
skills and competence

Growing children feel great pride each time they con-
quer something that they were not capable of achieving
previously. They spend so many years dependent in some
way or another that it gives them a sense of freedom and
autonomy when they at last grow tall enough, strong
enough, dextrous enough, and responsible enough to
manage themselves and undertake tasks that combine
skill and knowledge that can help others.

Boys tend to have strong spatial skills; they can see
how things fit together and can rearrange objects in
their minds. Many can easily remember information
about routes, maps, and blueprints, which helps make
them adept at building and mending things.

Practical skills help a boy to manage on his own. They
are valuable not so much for survival but because autonomy is the ultimate expression of self—the way all of us
experience ourselves. Competencies, then, help children
to be proactive, contribute to a fuller sense of identity,
and boost self-esteem.

Parents	Teachers

- Write down all the things your son is good at and likes to do. Think of ways you can put any of these skills to practical use in your home.

- If he is too young to be of genuine help, encourage him to come and hold things for you or to pass things, and he will learn at the same time.

- Give him any discarded bit of electrical appliance or other equipment (if safe) to take apart and explore.

- When a student mentions something he has done, made, or mended at home, compliment the skill involved: "Sounds like you're good at that sort of thing, Tom. Want a job at my house!?"

- As boys develop their manual dexterity, show how this can be put to practical use: "Wow. That would make you good at electronics/ tuning my guitar/dicing vegetables/getting my baby daughter dressed in the morning!"

40 | Go deeper—accept his fears and feelings

My biggest problem is my Dad who keeps saying, 'Be a man' every time I cry. I know I'm a boy but it's so hard to hold it in. I worry I'll be a failure with a capital F.

—Shawn, age 12

"When a child cannot be sad or lonely or angry because his parents will not be pleased with him if he is, he will feel he cannot be the person he knows himself to be and he will believe that he is unsatisfactory," writes psychotherapist Dorothy Rowe. A child whose fears and feelings are ignored or denied will not only feel misunderstood but also very alone. Apart from our psychological inheritance, it is our feelings that make us who we are and give us our sense of self. We experience these, often intensely, before we have the vocabulary to describe them, and they are our first building blocks. That certain things interest us, upset, frustrate, or hurt us, give us pleasure or make us defensive and selfish creates our individuality. If we can recognize all of a boy's particular moods and characteristics, we will demonstrate a deep understanding of him and how he sees his world.

If we accept a boy's dilemmas at his level, he will be spared the pain of isolation and the grief at having apparently lost his parents' support. He will be free to be and grow; nothing less.

Parents	Teachers

- Accept that your son's fearful beliefs are real to him. He should not be told that boys don't believe that nonsense and should not feel scared of things like monsters, the dark, or deep water.

- Notice his happy moods from his body movements, shining eyes, or bouncy walk, and say, "You seem very cheerful today. Something nice must have happened. Lucky you!" and let him keep it to himself if he doesn't want to tell you why.

- Notice his sad moods, too, and accept that he will feel angry, jealous, resentful, or lonely and even hate you, and tell him that's natural and okay. Never deny his difficult feelings.

- Some boys are very sensitive and squeamish. Prevent other children in the class from picking on anyone and teasing him for his natural feelings.

- Learning can be frightening. Accept that some reluctance to try could mask a deep fear of failure, and try to get to the bottom of this. The learning environment must be made safe for boys who lack confidence.

- Fears and feelings— indeed, all strong emotions—make learning difficult. Understand what a boy might be going through in his personal life, what pattern and expectation of relationships he brings into school, and consider how these may affect him.

Chapter 6

The Language of Praise:
Ways to Say It—and Give It

Human beings communicate in many subtle and less subtle ways. We use words, touch, facial expressions, and a range of different physical and symbolic gestures. We often merely sense the pleasure we have given others through the tone of voice they use or the way they look at us. We often interpret a number of reactions and piece together an overall impression. As adults, we don't always need to have praise spelled out every time that someone thinks we have done well.

If praise is valuable and worthwhile because it helps boys to feel acknowledged, noticed, approved of, valued, accepted, and appreciated as well as helps them to be successful, it follows that there are many ways to praise them. Praise does not always have to be given in words. Boys, too, as they mature, can appreciate the more subtle signs of praise and know we are grateful. Although language is what we tend to use to express our delight and surprise when a child has done well, by extending our praise repertoire we will limit the dangers already noted associated with spoken praise—and sometimes surprise them, which is always fun!

Children thrive when they are sure we enjoy their company, so it is important to have fun with them when they do well. We should not make fun of praise or make fun of them by being sarcastic when giving praise, but the whole family can have plenty of fun discovering different ways to express love and appreciation and finding approaches that are lighter in tone.

41 Keep approval simple

The more we spell it out, the more labored, false, inappropriate, or overdone the praise can become. To prevent a child from feeling burdened or uncomfortable and even misunderstood by our outpourings, we should, quite simply, keep our expressions of approval simple.

Approval, as has been explained, focuses on the individual. It puts the child in the spotlight, which is why he may squirm if it becomes exaggerated. Appreciation, on the other hand, relates to the task and therefore sometimes needs to be more detailed and specific (though still not disproportionate) so our child knows he can trust our appreciation.

Even praise that describes and offers a boy an account of what has pleased us (sometimes called *descriptive praise*) can be kept simple if we say things such as "Nice bike riding," "Well caught," or "Well tried" instead of "That was clever, how you cycled that tight circle." Leaving out some detail allows him to decide for himself what it was that was good and makes him less dependent on our assessment and freer to make up his own mind.

Parents	Teachers

- Vary the words, style, and response to avoid sounding like a stuck record. Children very quickly switch off and imagine the rest once they hear the intro, especially when we nag. Even repetitive praise begins to sound stale.

- Try such responses as "That's terrific!" "Brilliant!" "That's great!" "Thanks for doing that"; "That was sensible"; "How thoughtful!" and "What a great idea!"

- If your son begins to look at you askance instead of beaming with pride, go easy because you are probably overdoing it. Save your comments for something that matters more to him.

- Comments on written work need to be full and explicit, but spoken approval can be short: "I really liked that story/ your arguments/the line you took. Take a look at my comments."

- Warmer tones of voice and full-hearted attention convey approval, too.

Say it with a smile

Sometimes children don't need to hear anything spoken. Beaming smiles are enough. When they reach the finish line in a school race and turn around to see if we saw their effort or their triumph, a smile and a nod from a distance is all we can give—and it is often more than enough.

Parents	Teachers
• We can use store-bought smiley face stickers sparingly, as a surprise or reminder of our love, especially at times we cannot be there. But make no mistake: These will be no substitute for the real thing!	• Smiley faces given at the end of work show you are pleased with the result, but they don't offer useful, detailed feedback when that is more appropriate.
• For a younger boy, we can draw a simple smiley face on a blackboard in his bedroom after bedtime for him to find on waking. But beware of forgetting to do so if it has become a nightly routine!	

43 | Talk with touch

Touch has its own language. It can say so much in such a variety of ways, and it need only be fleeting. Touch is an intimate way to demonstrate an equality of regard and respect, for example. It can express feelings more quickly than words, and although it is less precise, it has the great advantage of allowing the receiver to read what he wants—and needs to hear—into it. It is therefore more likely to hit home and satisfy. Touch is certainly less open to misinterpretation than streams of worthy words and is an important gesture of approval, appreciation, and giving. Its capacity to convey understanding makes it also a useful way to demonstrate empathy.

A child who lives around adults who never touch him, even if they say the "right" praise words, could feel ignored, unworthy of attention, inferior, misunderstood, and, eventually, ashamed—the very opposite of what we hope praise will achieve.

Parents	Teachers
• Experiment with little touches of appreciation instead of using words.	• Of course it is not usually appropriate for professionals to touch male students, especially as they get older. Nevertheless, if you stand quite close while you look over a child's work, you can show him that he is acceptable and that you feel comfortable in his presence.
• If touch has disappeared from your relationship with your growing son, sit close to him as he watches TV, ruffle his hair when he comes in from school, or play with his hands and fingers as you chat with him at bedtime.	
• If he finds your approaches difficult, ask him beforehand so you know he feels ready for your attention.	• Consider whether shaking a boy's hand or giving him a high five is an alternative acceptable way to demonstrate approval and appreciation.

Use fun gestures

My teenage son did very well on some important exams. I wanted to show my appreciation and acknowledge his achievement without using money, gifts, or getting too heavy about it because he'd worked hard for his own satisfaction, not to please me. I bought a large sheet of stiff paper, selected a handful of cute photos from the family collection representing different stages of his life, and stuck these on, writing an amusing comment next to each one that made reference to his potential. He thought it was silly but funny, and he loved the gesture! He still has it, eight years later.

Money is not the only way to measure value or express pleasure, though it can be very easy to sign checks. Although boys love to get something new that they have longed for, they also appreciate being on the receiving end of an original gesture that takes time and special effort, something tailored to their passions that makes them laugh. They will almost certainly remember it for years to come.

Parents	Teachers
• Other fun gestures that can show our appreciation include — arranging a special outing as a treat — preparing his favorite meal — having a friend over for a sleepover — buying a new item for his room	• Games and prizes work well as an end-of-semester treat to recognize the class's collective progress. Simple prizes of candy, chocolate, or party bag gifts make it even more fun and special.

45 Hugs are for sharing

A hug is a physical gesture that enables us to share any feelings of joy or disappointment.

It is essentially nonjudgmental because it is empathic and it says, "I'm happy for you" as well as "I am sad or happy or pleased with you." It is a two-way gesture, for the hug has to be accepted and reciprocated. When it finishes, it leaves our son holding onto the feeling, and there is nothing we can take away from him and use for our benefit.

Some families don't feel comfortable with such physical closeness. They don't hug much or kiss or express themselves in other physical ways. And boys, as they enter their preteens or teens, often reject (particularly) maternal embraces. Passing on a hug to a pet dog or cat or to a soft toy that's an old favorite may be one way to make the gesture of embrace without forcing one on him.

Parents	Teachers
• "Here's a hug [and make the gesture]. When you're ready for it, come and get it!"	• Teachers cannot hug children, but they are able to stand close or pat an arm or shoulder instead or express their delight in words.
• "Are you in the mood to share your happiness? How about my giving you a hug, then?"	
• "That's made me really happy. Give me a hug so I can share it with you."	

Say it with surprises

Surprises are another way of saying thank you, or of showing appreciation or love. A favorite meal; a plate of pieces of fruit arranged as a funny face, a spaceship, or a rocket; a surprise outing; a balloon that you have written or drawn on; an unexpected small present—all are examples of surprises that can show appreciation of some special effort or simply to say how much you have enjoyed your child that week or weekend.

Friday treats are a lovely way to note the end of a school week. If any boy wants to know what the treat is "for," you can reply, "To mark the end of a week's work," or "Because you are you!"

Parents	Teachers
• Treats and surprises don't have to be earned or deserved.	• Curriculum pressures leave little space for surprises, but the end of a semester is a good moment to appreciate everyone's commitment and have fun.
• If a treat is laden with hard-to-earn parental approval, it could make a child anxious: "But what if I'm not good or successful next time?"	
• The pleasure is the surprise and the thought, not the object itself. It can be really simple— and cheap!	
• "Today, just for fun, we're going on a mystery night walk with flashlights!"	

47 Let him feel whatever he feels

My stepson returned from staying with his mother for a two-week vacation and seemed very down. I wanted him to feel good about returning to us. I couldn't ignore his mood, although the implications were uncomfortable. So I said to him, "It must be really hard for you. When you're with Dad you want to be with Mom, and when you're with Mom, a bit of you wants to be with Dad." He replied, "Yeah."

Affirmation means we accept a boy as he is, not some version of the person we want him to be. A boy who does well and thrives (for these are not the same things) is someone who knows himself and feels free to "be." If he feels it's all right to feel sad, frustrated, happy, disappointed, angry, hateful, confident, frightened, or excited, he will probably see his parents' tolerance, continuing presence, and love throughout all these emotions as a sign that he can trust them and himself because they accept and trust all of him. He will feel understood, and if given the scope to decide when he will pull out all the stops, when he will coast, when he will explore his developing interests, and how he will allocate his time, he will be sufficiently confident to manage these activities sensibly.

Parents	Teachers
• Our feelings are the building blocks of ourselves.	• Acknowledge boys' feelings, but ensure that the rules about acceptable ways for them to be expressed are maintained.
• Allow your son to feel disappointed or angry if he doesn't do well—or if anything that you say is not well received.	
• If you take the time and trouble to understand the feelings that may explain his behavior, you will find out more about him.	
• It is normal for boys to feel angry, insulted, hostile, and proud, for boys are, like us, whole human beings. Ask yourself why his reactions bother you; don't put pressure on him to deny or ignore them.	

48 | Allow him to say it

It is not necessarily pigheaded or offensively arrogant for a child to believe he has done well and to admit it. Indeed, secondary-school students are increasingly encouraged to judge the quality of their own work as part of well-organized self-assessment programs. Many nursery schools invite children as young as three to "plan, do, then review" the effectiveness of their chosen approaches to various tasks.

The possible downside of openly admitting to having been successful is pride and conceit. Children quickly identify "stuck-up" braggers and can turn against them ruthlessly; indeed, most children possess a deep-seated reticence about their talents and are not natural boasters. Perhaps those that do boast are simply copying their parents! But the danger is avoided if we make clear that a boy's particular abilities do not make him better as a person than someone without those talents and that he should never look down on anyone who performs differently. Of course he should be openly joyful about his success within the family, but it is best if he does not make a fuss about it among his friends.

Parents	Teachers

Parents

- Teach that "good at" means "different from" not "better than" in anything other than the skill in question.

- Always ask, "Are you pleased with it?" or "Would you praise this?" and let your son decide and say it.

- Boys tend to overestimate their work in self-assessment. If your son says it's great and he's really happy with it, ask what he might do differently next time to make it even better. He'll then be forced to look for any room for improvement.

Teachers

- "I was very happy with this. Well done. Did you think you'd done it well?"

- Encourage self-assessment, backed up with peer review and peer moderation.

- Before you fill out report cards, ask students to anticipate your remarks. If there is a major discrepancy between your view and a student's, in either direction, discuss it with him later.

49 Let siblings in on it

It should be part of living in a family that siblings value and appreciate each others' particular achievements. Praise shouldn't always be issued from the top down. But this won't happen without everyone's first having heard you say, "Well done," or "That's a lovely . . . ," simple phrases that are easy for all children to use. Whereas no child should have to assume a parent's responsibility for affirming or accepting a brother or sister, each child will feel more generous and open with praise (and less threatened by or possessive of it) when praise is not treated as a treasured winner's cup or an advantage to exploit.

Difficulties can arise when one sibling has talents or inclinations that enable him to be more enthusiastic and successful than another. He may then attract more admiration from friends and family, creating an imbalance with his siblings. If this happens, ask the surrounding admirers to cool off; let the active brother learn to enjoy the pleasure he gains from his commitments and not seek other people's praise; and make sure that the other siblings receive plenty of loving attention and appreciation, often more nourishing than accolades. Tensions, jealousies, and rivalries between siblings tend to appear either when one of them receives preferential attention (so seems to be the regular favorite) or when the line between the achievement and the child becomes blurred.

Parents	Teachers

- Show joy in each of your children's varied milestones, pleasures, and personalities.

- Younger children can draw a picture as an appreciative gesture for a brother. Older ones can say, "Well done," ask about the event, and watch the play, game, or performance.

- Share praise all around. Don't allow one child in particular to get all your acclaim and attention. If jealousy becomes expressed destructively, the balance you seek to achieve in your home will be upset.

- Be sensitive to the amount of flattering feedback a talented child receives. View it as "his chosen thing" rather than as anything remarkable.

- Positively value each child as an individual.

- Raise the suggestion that a sibling in the same school might be pleased to know about some special outcome.

- Beware of telling a brother or sister about a sibling's good efforts, in case your comment is misinterpreted as an underhanded incentive to improve.

Praise should focus more on the event or the child than on us. Once we start sentences with *I* the emphasis becomes our view of things: "I like the way . . . "; "I'm very pleased . . . "; "I think you could have done more to . . . "; "I was so surprised you did so well"; "I am convinced everything will go well for you because you have prepared so thoroughly." The earlier discussion of the purpose of praise highlighted such things as acknowledgment, attention, and affirmation. Children love to please their parents when they are young, but as they get older they need less of their parents' pleasure and more affirmation and confirmation that they have judged things well and are on the right track, which will encourage confidence.

If a boy is hungry for praise, he will find any format rewarding, including all *I* phrases, but these won't help to wean him off an unhealthy reliance on our judgment. If he starts to sense that he is being manipulated or too closely monitored, he may simply ignore all praise. On the other hand, phrases such as "You did really well," "That was a great result," and "The way you were able to reflect on that test paper and spot where you went wrong was impressive" are more focused on the process and are statements of fact that center on him, not of judgment that center on you.

Parents	Teachers

Parents

- "You are terrific as you are, *and* you're extra special to me!" is less loaded than "I love you as you are"—especially if he has just done something to please you.

- "You handled that really well. Others might have lost their cool. Well done!" is preferable to "I really liked the way you handled that."

- "You're such fun to be around" is less of a burden to carry than "I love being around you when you're this cheerful."

- Free him: Focus your remarks on his ability to plan out tasks well rather than offering your opinion on the outcome.

Teachers

- "You've clearly got the measure of this problem now. This was a terrific assignment and shows what you are really capable of" is more convincing than "I am pleased you have understood this problem and done this piece of work so well."

Chapter 7

Common Mistakes to Try to Avoid

Despite our best intentions to help boys do well and show how much we love and appreciate them, we can still say either the wrong thing entirely or the right thing but at the wrong time (or in the wrong way), and through clumsiness or ignorance, we can put our foot in our mouth.

Though it may surprise some people, the worst offense is not necessarily criticism, some of which may be justified and valuable. It is not helpful to protect our child from every nuance of disapproval or disappointment. When he has misjudged or failed to understand things or ignored clear guidance, he should receive straightforward yet constructive, supportive explanations of what he can do differently next time. Constructive criticism is a far more helpful response than alternatives such as harsh punishment, scathing sarcasm, turning a "blind eye," or even offering excessive praise for effort when the outcome is way below expectation—and your son knows it. These can all have counterproductive consequences and are explored in this chapter.

The dangers that are associated with the wrong kind of attention, be it indiscriminate praise or constant criticism, include perfectionism (explored in Chapter 10), stress-inducing pressure, burnout and opting out, and, perhaps curiously, feelings of low self-worth. We might intend that our son feel pride and satisfaction, but this is not guaranteed. These outcomes, admittedly, lie at the extreme end; signs of interim difficulty or more serious trouble ahead can include secretiveness, mild cheating, copying other children's work, and learned helplessness.

The characteristic common to all the mistakes reviewed here is placing our concerns and desires before our son's feelings and wishes: a failure to treat him as an autonomous human being. Each child should be allowed to be who he is and not be compared to anyone else. He should not be used by us as a vehicle to make good on any missed childhood opportunities of our own that we may now regret. He should be given the freedom to say no or stop and should be offered every opportunity to do well for his own pleasure, not simply to please us. Parents often need to step in temporarily to help a child over a rough patch—for example, when he doesn't understand a math problem or gets disenchanted with his progress on a musical instrument and wants to give up—but when he has overcome the problem, we should withdraw, allowing him from then on to set his own pace and direction.

51 | Think about why you're offering praise

When we consider whether to give what we may see as the "gift" of praise, we look first at what our child has done and whether the behavior or circumstance warrants it. Our focus is therefore on him and is context-bound and time-limited: The conscious part of our attention is fixed on him. But less obvious ulterior motives often lurk behind our apparently altruistic actions or comments that have more to do with us—our dreams, desires, and fears—than with him. We applaud certain attributes to help him achieve aims we consider desirable. We can so easily try to turn him into what we want him to be.

At one level, this is inevitable. Of course it is a parent's job to encourage socially acceptable behavior and discourage actions that will set him back or get him into trouble. We do shape children's behavior and should do so, as gardeners prune growing plants to develop stronger stems and larger flowers. But we should also take care neither to take a cutting from ourselves and graft it onto our children nor to cut and style so much that they need walls or wires to hold them up. We should not contrive to boost our own vulnerable self-worth with our son's success but instead give him the autonomy he needs even if this means he does not reach the future we might have hoped for him.

Parents	Teachers

Parents

- Think about whether you are making a point of being positive to compensate for being very preoccupied recently, or whether you could you be saying "the right things" to make him feel more loving toward you because you need more support.

- If the answer to either of these is yes, or even possibly, beware of your motives. Better to address the issue directly or at its source.

- Watch carefully how he responds to the different ways in which you express approval and delight.

- As much as you can, put it back to him: "Yes, I do like it, but the more important thing is whether you do"; "To me, you did very well, but were you pleased with the result?"

Teachers

- If praise is natural, it will roll off the tongue without much forethought.

- Individual boys who are despondent may need more encouragement than others.

Good is such a bad word when it comes to ensuring that praise is effective. It is bad because it is inadequate, for it says so little. It is a shorthand word used to convey many things and sometimes some not very helpful things. Boys may infer from hearing the catchall term that it refers to them, not their actions.

One use of the word *good* is "Good, you did what I wanted you to do, and you behaved in the way I hoped you would." A good child may therefore tend to be passive: He is not noisy, boisterous, messy, curious, or clumsy. He does his work assiduously. He is that particular parent's perfect child. And that's the point. Boys who are required to be good and are then rewarded amply can lose their sense of individuality as they fill the mold shaped by specific parental expectations.

The opposite of good is bad: They are black and white words—and, more damagingly, black *or* white words. When a "good" boy is being less obliging, or just behaving normally, he will often be called "bad," which is neither fair nor beneficial to his learning.

Parents	Teachers

- Instead of *good* we can say *clever, organized, thoughtful, helpful,* or *creative* or just say, "You're a happy boy." If your son has done something he's pleased with, that's how he'll be feeling.

- Instead of labeling him "bad" or "naughty," we should turn it around to our view: "That seems to me rather selfish," or "I didn't like that behavior." In this context, it is preferable to use *I* rather than *you.*

- If we want to convey in simple terms our delight in his existence, we can say, "Mmm. You're my lovable boy!" the prerequisite for self-esteem.

- Boys who do most of what you ask but hold a bit of themselves back are good enough!

- "Very good" on a piece of work tells the student very little about what he did right. Instead you could write, "Very well argued," "Very well researched," "Very good use of detail," or "Lovely descriptions—I saw it all!"

- "Good" boys should be not so good to teach. Good students should always question and challenge.

53 Don't turn your dream into his success—or nightmare

A ten-year-old boy who had just been selected to dance with a national ballet company after an intense competition against other budding ballet stars was asked whether he was pleased with the result. He replied, "My mother will be pleased."

Being successful does not necessarily generate psychological health and confidence. When children are required to carry and make a reality of their parents' dreams, they are not usually free to take things in a direction or at a pace that suits them, to mix and match their free-time activities to create a better balance, or to decide when they have had enough. For success to create confidence and security rather than anxiety and insecurity, boys must believe they are following their own wishes. Fathers must be aware that their son's Sunday football game is just for fun and not a way to make up for their own near miss at getting onto a league team. Be clear, for example, that a son should embark on tennis lessons to explore his talents and for enjoyment, rather than to fulfill his parents' dream or, worse, to generate generous prize money for his family's personal financial gain.

Parents	Teachers

Parents

- Boys are not puppets—they are growing people.

- "Who is he doing it for—for him or for me?" is a very important question that should be asked at every stage of a boy's progress if he is performing competitively. And answer it honestly.

- Don't compete with, criticize, or ridicule him. Every challenge drags him into your territory and reinforces his belief that your view and preferences must be better.

- Give him room to be himself. It's your problem, not his, if you feel uncomfortable with his preferred interests and direction.

Teachers

- Vary your teaching style and lessons. Your comfort zones, passions, and communication methods may not suit all the boys in your class.

- Encourage tolerance and mutual respect for difference among all students so they learn not to impose their values and choices on others.

54 Don't take credit for his success

Sometimes parents invest so much of their time and effort in helping their son to achieve the hoped-for success that they are convinced it could never have been achieved without them. They may have spent hours coaching him or sacrificed a great deal to pay for a private tutor. They may have imposed strict practice regimes or been genuinely supportive when something went awry so that their child was able to find his own way back to confidence. Such actions enable parents to take responsibility for their son's success, expressed either privately or openly, which can then undermine their son's contribution. Offering rewards and incentives can have the same effect, making parental intervention the critical factor in a son's success. When parents steal some of the credit, which is what providing an incentive can amount to, a child may feel empty and used simply as a tool to boost a parent's self-esteem.

Comments such as "I told you that you were a 'natural.' That's why I signed you up for the course"; and "Congratulations for making the team. Aren't you pleased now that I put you on that healthier diet?" clearly claim some of the credit for the parent.

Parents	Teachers

- Pass your possible contribution over to your son: "You became so much more organized; well done"; "You started to look after yourself and care about your health, and it really paid off"; "You took real advantage of the extra experience that course gave you"; "You've developed a lovely relationship with books, and it may well have helped."

- If your friend's son does particularly well at something, it is more appropriate to focus on the boy's pleasure than to attribute any of the success to your friend and congratulate her. Instead, say: "I hear Juan did really well; he must be delighted."

- Credit the class or individual, not yourself. If you helped, that is no more than your professional duty.

- "I was just the fertilizer— you put down the roots and did the growing!"

55 | "I'm so proud of you!"

Which of the following would you be most likely to say? "I'm really proud of you for managing that!" "I hope you feel proud of yourself for doing that—you deserved to do well after all that effort"; "You probably feel really proud to have achieved that"; "I feel so proud of you and proud to have you as my child".

When I talked to a group of fifteen-year-old boys, they all agreed that the parental phrase they most love to hate was "I'm so proud of you." They found it hard to explain why this response grated so much, but the problem seemed to relate to its being "over the top" as well as causing discomfort with having a parent too emotionally involved in their work. They did not want the responsibility for delivering or maintaining their parent's sense of pride, and they certainly had not worked hard for a particular test or exam in order that their parent could feel that way—they had done it for themselves and for their own reasons.

Our role should be to enable our son to feel proud of himself, independently and regardless of our feelings because he knows what he set out to achieve and how much effort he applied.

Parents	Teachers

- Keep comments as free from judgment as possible. "You probably felt really proud when you heard that" implies that if he did feel that, you can understand why. If not, no matter.

- Even "I hope you feel proud of that result" implies that if he doesn't, he should because your view counts.

- Pride can be an unjustified opinion: Be careful you're not exaggerating his achievement.

- Pride might, indeed, come before a fall if, as a result of your insistence that he excel in one activity, he decides to avoid the pressure and drop it.

- You can be proud of the achievement of a class— proud of everyone or of your professional input. But your pride is of no relevance to any individual's success.

- "I am really impressed with your progress," "You deserve to feel proud of your achievement," and "I'm so pleased you have understood things and can now work closer to your true ability level" are more appropriate remarks for individual boys.

56 Keep it clean: no sarcasm or caveats

Ninety-nine percent. That's not bad! But why did you let one get away?

When adults are uncomfortable with giving praise, they often lace it with something rather nasty—a sting or kickback—to qualify and downgrade the compliment and make it not quite the generous gesture it might have been. This is a sufficiently common practice so that it has been given a name: *contaminative praise.* It can become a style or habit, is sometimes dressed up as humor, and is not always said to hurt; yet it usually does. The child is not quite let off the hook and still needs to wait for the full approval that frees him to move on.

Contaminative praise is probably uncomfortably familiar. Examples of such comments include: "This report card is great, but why did you have to take so long to mend your ways?" "That model is really lovely—no one would know you used to be all fingers and thumbs!" "Your bedroom looks so much tidier now; terrific, but it won't stay this way long—you'll see!"

Parents	Teachers

- Imagine praise as a cookie: Would you give your son a cookie as a reward and then, just as he reaches for it, pull it back, shake salt onto it, and return it to him to eat? Of course not. So why would you effectively do that with praise?

- Sarcasm is traditionally said to be the lowest form of wit.

- If you see it as harmless fun, reflect on the essence of humor. Is making jokes at other people's expense—especially children who won't see it the same way—the only way to have fun and make others laugh?

- Sarcasm is neither an effective nor a professional tool for teachers. It should never be used as it confuses and humiliates children.

Absence makes children's hearts grow harder

My two-year-old son was looked after during the day by a neighbor's daughter for two months when I took a short-term job. She was warm and wonderful, devising many great things for him to do. But then she went off to college. She turned on the charm and enthusiasm very naturally on her first return visit, and he loved it. But after each absence he was increasingly confused and then actually turned away and refused to engage with her.

For adults, so the saying goes, absence makes the heart grow fonder. This is not the case for children, however, who find unexpected or long absences due to work trips or hospitalization much harder to understand and endure. Young children, in particular, are likely to feel at least a little bit abandoned, unwanted, or at fault when, for example, they start day care and it is unfamiliar. This is largely because young children are extremely egocentric and often believe the absence must be a punishment for a wrongdoing: The very young frequently make sense of information and experience in unexpected ways.

We sometimes cover our guilt for periods of unplanned or unusually frequent absences by being extra attentive to our children or by overrewarding them when we return. This may console and convince younger boys for a while, but older ones may feel manipulated, remain confused and skeptical, and prefer to maintain a safer emotional distance that makes them resistant to praise. Boys will accept praise more readily from people they feel they can trust.

Parents	Teachers
• If you have to be away frequently, develop clear and predictable routines and rituals that mark your comings and goings so your son can learn to trust your love despite your absence.	• If you have had to take time off from the classroom at unpredictable moments, don't expect your feedback to have quite the same positive impact when you return. It takes time to rebuild the trust.
• Try not to be overexuberant when you come home, especially if you expect to be away again soon or to be very preoccupied (which can amount to the same thing). A calm, close, intimate cuddle may be more effective than bellows of delight with presents showered down on him.	• Boys who have felt rejected and constantly criticized or manipulated by their parents may reject any form of appreciation or approval from their teachers because they will find it hard to accept it as truth.
	• For disbelieving students, select one thing only to comment on positively and mention this six times every day. Eventually, he will begin to see himself differently and accept that he is worthy of appreciation.

58 Accentuate the positive— but notice the negative

It is fine to accentuate the positive, especially when boys are young and boisterous and get into lots of scrapes and sometimes cannot help being clumsy or physical; but as they get older the negative should increasingly be noticed, not ignored. Young children make lots of mistakes either of judgment or about their physical capacity. It is hard for them to think ahead because rules are hard to grasp or because they get tired and fractious or need attention. We should understand and tolerate these errors that cannot really be considered "naughty," and we should certainly not punish them. At a period of life when mistakes and accidents abound a boy should be allowed to start his life feeling positive, capable, and confident, not cowed by constant criticism and failure.

But by the time boys reach the age of seven or eight, the negatives should be noted and addressed. "Accentuate the positive" means, essentially, to emphasize helpful behavior and to make it conspicuous, but that does not mean we should ignore outrageous behavior or go overboard with exaggerated praise when the event is modest.

Parents	Teachers

- You might say, "I love going with you to the store, but this time it was not fun. It's not okay for you to go on and on about having something to eat or to nag about missing your TV show. You're usually great company, but I'll think about going alone if it happens again."

- A boy said, "I prefer to hear, 'At least you tried hard, even if you didn't do so well,' rather than 'That was good,' which wouldn't be true."

- "It clearly matters to you that you came in fifth today. Was there a special reason you wanted to do better?" is preferable to "But darling, you did just great, so don't get so upset!"

- "'That was okay. But if you do it this way next time, you might find it easier' is better than an outright complaint," said one fourteen-year-old boy, "because it leaves me feeling okay."

59 Don't compare him to others

When our boys are babies, it is natural for all of us to look for similarities between our brand-new infant and our partner, any siblings, or other relatives, so that everyone feels he is part of the family immediately. Not long after, however, the comparisons with others can become far less benign.

Comments such as "Your brother would not have dreamed of behaving like that"; "Why can't you be an A student like your sister?" or "Dylan eats everything when he comes here. Why are you so picky?" can be upsetting. Those who lived with such taunts say that they were far from being a spur to action; these people's childhood was tainted by them.

Even handing out equal praise or favorable comparisons can act as a brake. Saying, "Jerry's the brain box and Sam's the family athlete", may give each boy something to be proud of but limits the likelihood that either will explore his full talent in the other's special sphere. And comparisons with parents of the "You take after me" variety can be dangerous, too. You may have been a budding musician and played in local concerts at the same age your son is performing, but let his achievement go unsullied by his inheritance. Any boy will want to be himself and not likened to anyone else.

Parents	Teachers

- Each child will respond in his own individual way to a situation because he is unique. Comparisons may stunt his development and undermine his confidence in himself.

- Make it clear there is room for more than one mathematician, pianist, or soccer player in the family.

- Don't compare your son with how you were or what you did at his age. He is himself, not you, and you've probably embellished the memory!

- Labeling makes children resentful and can tempt them to do the opposite out of spite.

- See each child as an individual, not in the context of his family. Never compare him to a sibling to disparage, coerce, or even praise work.

- The most useful, and constructive, comparison to make is with his own previous work or performance.

- Be especially supportive of the originality and creativity through which he is exploring and expressing his difference.

60 | Don't swamp him with your success

Acorns seldom grow under the great oak.

If we want our son to be able gradually to recognize when he's done well and be open about his pleasure in his accomplishments rather than rely on us for warm words, we can set an example by describing occasions when things go well for us. However, it is possible for parents to go too far and swamp their son with their success. It is important to leave room for him to feel that small advances are worthwhile and valuable and to avoid implying that each child has to excel to fit in—or otherwise suffer derision or rejection.

Where parental success is paraded, it can create an impossible act for boys to follow. Though many sons follow in their father's or mother's footsteps and are happy to do so, legions of others get put off by the anticipated competition and feel intimidated by any expectation of matching parental achievements. Do we suggest to our boys that we are better as a person for our success and feel superior (a dangerous implication), or do we instead explain our success as the result of hard work, luck, and embracing opportunity? If we do the latter, we are less likely to arouse complex reactions, resentments, and fears.

Parents	Teachers

- Handle your own success with sensitivity. Convey surprise rather than worthiness, and attribute it to judgment, hard work, and good fortune, not genius.

- Any significant success of yours will be evident; there'll be no need to blow your own horn.

- Don't strive to excel at everything. Doing something well enough, and sometimes not quite making it, sets a healthier example.

- Where two parents are successful in different fields, boys can have difficulty finding their own niche. So value his particular strengths, and parents shouldn't compete with each other, either!

- When a boy struggles with a problem of understanding, it won't help him if you declare that it is really very simple and then explain it to him again in the same way and at the same speed.

- Ask if anyone in the class is willing to describe how he made sense of the task or procedure.

- Underachieving boys will be motivated by the successful efforts of other strugglers, not by the success of the class star.

Chapter 8

Bribes, Rewards, and Incentives

When parents of boys get together, they often swap stories about their sons' laziness and disorganization—especially when it comes to finishing school projects or homework before a looming deadline. Many boys seem less switched on by academic work than girls, would much prefer to be outside playing ball, and are generally inclined to leave everything until the last minute. Many seem totally unconcerned by personal untidiness and are indifferent to the state of their bedrooms. We can tear our hair out with frustration and become desperate in our search for opportunities to change their ways that we see as barriers to their achieving success.

Offering a bribe is the one tactic many parents resort to in order to nudge their sons into action. Although most people call them bribes, they are more correctly described as inducements, given in the form of incentives and rewards. A "bribe" is something offered to persuade someone to do something illegal or wrong; what we generally offer is an incentive to persuade our child to undertake something legal and desirable—and, usually, in his own interest—that otherwise he would not do. Perhaps we use the term *bribe* because we feel some guilt about what we're doing or because we consider it a last resort and wish it weren't necessary.

Incentives and rewards can work well, but they can also lead to problems or become a problem themselves. They must be used very carefully, especially as boys grow older. When boys are young, tactics such as using star charts and stickers to mark progress can help impatient youngsters with short time horizons see their progress represented visually, and the same tactics can help boisterous, impulsive boys control their strong desires. But even five-year-olds can get fresh and argue about whether a particular target has or has not been reached or debate how many stars a notable success deserves. The truth is that we often use incentives to engineer a particular outcome that we consider desirable. If incentives are overused, boys can end up feeling entangled by the rewards and affronted that we don't trust them to manage any challenge on their own, making them question our belief in them.

There is no obvious age after which rewards and incentives are best avoided altogether. It is more important to consider each child's personality and maturity, the problem at hand, and how successfully rewards have been used in the past. However, the closer children are to college and work, the more they need to motivate themselves.

Be clear about the purpose

I don't want any money to make me practice my trumpet. If I wanted to play it more often, I'd do it anyway!

—Jeremy, age 10

Incentives come in various forms and send various messages. There is the "sweeten the pill" incentive, which we use to show we realize that something is difficult. We might say, "I can see that you might run out of steam because this is quite a challenge. When you're through, I'll give you something to show I appreciate what you've done."

There is the "kick in the rear" incentive that says, in effect, "I'm not sure you'll do it without something to tempt you." For example, you might offer him a hundred dollars if he manages to reach the age of sixteen without smoking.

There is also the negative or threatening incentive. Instead of offering some prize, the inducement is to avoid experiencing an outright penalty or even simply not receiving something the boy would otherwise have. A parent might say, "Unless you improve your grade average, I won't pay for your driving lessons the way I did for your brother," or "If you don't quit teasing your sister, I'll take away all your action hero toys."

Parents	Teachers
• Remember, boys don't like to be manipulated. Think carefully about whether you really need to offer an incentive or if an alternative approach may be more suitable, such as showing interest in a project or offering to hear a daily progress report.	• Think whether any incentive you offer will help a boy to do his best, or whether you offer it to improve your overall results.
• Consider the importance of the particular outcome or target in question. If it marks a crucial turning point or if something important hangs on it, there may be more reason to ensure he will do his very best.	
• Ask whether he wants or needs to have the added boost of a reward or incentive. He could now be old enough to realize this is important and meet the challenge without help.	

62   Rewards are more effective as surprises

My Dad doesn't often praise me so it really means something when he does. But as soon as he does, I spot the opportunity and try to get some money out of him. I usually succeed.

—Max, age 15

A reward can be agreed to in advance as an incentive, or it can be offered afterward, produced as a surprise to express our appreciation. Rewards are most helpful and enjoyable if they are not announced in advance for two reasons: Given in this way, they prevent any unpleasant negotiation about whether the suggested reward is big enough; the chance is also reduced that any boy will intentionally underperform in order to keep the incentives coming.

My grandmother, brought up over a century ago, used to warn all of her grandchildren, "I want doesn't get." It was a typical Edwardian homily, designed to warn children against covetousness. Surprises that aren't dangled beforehand are more spontaneous and far less open to manipulation by parent or child.

Parents	Teachers

- Keep a reward as a genuine surprise. A financial reward that is pried out of you afterward is not a surprise. Praise is a form of reward. We generally reject the practice of double punishment, so why should we be so open to double rewards?

- In order to retain our gesture as a surprise, it follows that we cannot produce rewards too often.

- Surprises do not have to cost money. But the more toys and goods children possess, the harder it can be to find simple ways to please them. Examples could include cooking together, letting him use something of yours that he covets, or staying up late one weekend.

- Giving surprises to individual students could lay a teacher open to charges of favoritism. However, activities that students enjoy, such as having extra time on the computer, can be offered as a surprise reward.

63 Keep targets manageable: Ask whether he can realistically deliver

Children like to work with adults who have confidence in them and ask them to stretch, because that is when they give their best effort and make progress. Doing well when the challenge is easy is neither exciting nor rewarding. But challenges must be set to tempt children to develop themselves, not put them off because the challenges are overly ambitious or seem threatening. A target set too high is as unhelpful as one set too low.

We know that a target or expectation is realistic when the boy involved agrees that it is achievable. If his view is more pessimistic than ours, he may reject the objective and the reward before he starts. We should never set our child up to fail. If goals appear to him consistently unrealistic, the reward will never be earned, which could lead either to a disenchanted and more self-doubting child (who then refuses to engage at all) or to a heated argument about how close he got and what other recognition he might deserve given the advance he did achieve.

Parents	Teachers
• Ask your son what he thinks he can handle.	• Make sure the goal, deadline, and expectations are clear.
• Help him to devise clear plans to meet his goal.	• Help boys to assess whether the conditions have been met and to face the consequences, if not.
• If he seeks an easier target, start there and work up. Self-belief, so important to long-term striving, must be securely in place.	• If you detect overconfidence, ask for a detailed study plan—don't say he won't make it.
• Boys tend to overestimate their ability and do not usually pitch low to get an easier ride. If your son is pessimistic, it could signify fragile confidence.	• Don't constantly move the goalposts. Ask whether he's ready for the next challenge or needs some time for everything to sink in.
• Encourage him to mix short- and long-term goals.	

Reward him with your presence, not presents

My Dad often gives me money when I do well, but I prefer it if instead he takes me out somewhere. Then I have him all to myself.

—Reggie, age 14

Rewards are used, typically, as a sign that we appreciate what our son did and to encourage him. Another good reason for using rewards is that they give children little boosts along the otherwise endless journey that is growing and learning.

Children seem naturally materialistic. They catch on very quickly to how much things cost and are hawkish as they watch and assess whether a sibling or, especially, a stepsibling gets better gifts than they do. But they are also hardwired to detect insincerity or superficial gestures. They know how easy it is for many—though not all—parents to buy something. The best way to show that we truly appreciate their effort is to put some effort into our gesture, which means sharing our scarcest resource: time. Our time with our boys will genuinely encourage them; will demonstrate genuine appreciation, regard, and approval; and has infinite, not specific, value.

Parents	Teachers
• Depending on his age, watch him do something he enjoys, sit with him while he eats, chat as he falls asleep, give him a ride to a friend's, or play a game together.	• Find a moment to have a special quiet conversation that details his achievement and shows you are interested in and value him as an individual.
• Quiet time together can be as important as action-packed time. Turn off your cell phone!	• A personal touch could be to relate the current work to something he wrote previously.
• Give more generously of your time if there have been any family difficulties recently, as he may be unsettled and will almost certainly need you more.	• Point out what this good piece of work means for his future potential.
• If you're a nonresident parent, after he's had a big success make a special effort to keep any promise to visit or go out to celebrate.	

65 Let him help to choose the treat or incentive

Letting our son choose his incentive will lessen the possibility that he may see it as a surreptitious attempt by us to control him. It is a celebration on his terms.

If we choose the treat, we have to guess what he would like, and we might get it wrong. If he helps to choose the treat, it can still be a nice surprise. After a pleasing outcome, we can say he deserves a treat, and he can help to select it, while we give some guidance as to the appropriate scale of the gift or event.

With his treat, he can feel like a king, receiving special attention for a short while, which will contrast strongly with his daily diet of school, where he has to fall into line and be one of a very large crowd.

Parents	Teachers
• The choice of a treat will necessarily vary according to a boy's age. It could be a little toy, some candy, an extra story at bedtime, something that relates to a hobby, choosing the destination for a special trip out, watching a DVD just with you, or choosing the menu for a celebratory meal.	• There is less room for choice in a classroom context, but rather than determine what the treat should be, if there is some scope for choice it should be offered.

66 Money talks—back, so take care if you use it

Children often argue about the size of the reward they deserve and push for more. What was intended as a generous gesture can degenerate into a battle of wits and power. "I'll do it for ten dollars, not for five" is a not unfamiliar cry in households where money talks loudly and is used to ensure that parental will prevails. Even small children can barter over the appropriate payment for being good at the dentist.

To negotiate every penny is an obvious way to take control in a situation in which a boy senses financial manipulation. And if money is always accorded value as a reward, and more value than time, it may also become something a boy could desire strongly—and take—if he ever feels ignored and resentful. When money talks, it implies that spending is best, money buys influence, and money matters more than time or relationships.

Adolescent boys may be especially prone to wager and raise the stakes with their moms. If they associate masculinity with power and power with money, which many boys do, they're more likely to want to beat their mom at the money game than any dad who plays it.

Parents	Teachers

- If you hear, "My friends all got two hundred dollars for doing well," don't automatically cough up the money. His real reward is discovering later that life's best rewards are rarely financial.

- Lack of money may be a suitable temporary excuse, but if this is your main reason for not offering a financial reward, once the situation eases don't be surprised if he appears, hand held out.

- In class discussion time, ask for students' views about the value of money as a reward.

- Point out that the more money children receive via financial rewards, the less they need: Unless the amount rises, the incentive becomes progressively devalued.

- Reflect on how much you value your job because of or despite the money you receive.

Don't let money become the family's emotional currency

My dad's very generous when it comes to birthday presents. Sometimes he goes too far, and I wonder if he's trying to make up for not being around much.
—Ethan, age 17

No boy should ever feel that the bigger the present or the more money he is given, the more he is loved. Love cannot and should not be measured by price tags. How much you love a child should never become linked to how much money you are prepared to spend on him. When effort, commitment, and love become closely equated with money and costly gifts, children can ask for ever bigger gifts and use emotional blackmail to get them.

This occurs when gifts are used to fill emotional or time gaps in relationships or when they are purchased either to say sorry or to assuage guilt. Of course all dads and moms like to buy a little gift after a trip away, but if it stops being a surprise and becomes an expectation, we have to take stock. Any complaint along the lines that something more was expected because the trip has been a long one will show it is time to think afresh about how we make up for any time they miss with us.

Parents	Teachers
• When financial rewards become emotional currency, children can think, "Prove you're really pleased by giving me more," or "I did it anyway, but hey, let's lay on some guilt and see what happens!"	• If boys are used to relationships at home that are conditional and based on trading, they may try the same with you. Understand where this might come from, and be quiet and firm rather than angry.
• Stand up for yourself: Don't let your son exploit your love, and ensure that he knows, through the little things that you do and say, that you love him without proving it through giving presents.	
• If you feel guilty about frequent absence, talk to him directly about how sad this makes you and call him as regularly as you can at an agreed-on time so he knows he is "kept in mind." Presents will then be less necessary.	

Where motivation rests upon extrinsic guilt or pressure, there is less sense of self-determination.
—Howard Hall, professor of sports sciences

Psychological theory distinguishes between "intrinsic" and "extrinsic" rewards. Extrinsic rewards are those that exist outside the child, for example, money, toys, new clothes, or perhaps the present of a pet. *The Concise Oxford Dictionary* defines *extrinsic* as "not belonging to, not essential."

Internal, or intrinsic, rewards, by contrast, belong naturally to us. They lie inside each of us as positive thoughts and experiences and can be thought of as essential. Examples of internal rewards are pride and pleasure; a satisfied curiosity or a sense of mastery and capability; feeling fit, healthy, and agile. Rewards are usually posed to offer encouragement and to increase motivation, yet we know the most effective motivation is self-motivation. We all have to learn to do things because we want to, because we enjoy the self-satisfaction that usually flows from effort, progress, and achievement. Boys need to learn to acknowledge and value these feelings and consider them a sufficient reward. Boys' tendency to separate themselves from their feelings could make them rely more heavily on external rewards.

Parents	Teachers

- When something goes well, ask your son how he feels, so he learns to "read" and acknowledge the internal benefits of making an effort and doing himself justice.

- External rewards depend on others; they pale as they become predictable and eventually become mere tokens of success. To remain effective incentives, they have to increase.

- Internal rewards, by contrast, are within each person's control. If the pleasure of success fades, your son simply raises the target.

- Try to ensure that each boy understands and feels comfortable inside with the grade given or the comment made and that he has learned something.

- Make sure the benefit is doing well, not simply receiving the accolade or the bonus points. The older boys get, the more they like to gamble with manipulative games with rewards, and they may get hooked.

If rewards backfire, drop them

Rewards and incentives may backfire for several reasons. A boy may simply refuse to accept them; he may argue endlessly about the nature of the reward; or he may stop just short of the agreed-on achievement and still demand the reward. If a tactic is no longer working or has turned sour, how should we respond?

The first action is to stop using rewards altogether, rather than trying to devise another that may work better. The next step is to reflect on why this strategy has become a problem. It could be that the boy wants to show that he doesn't need rewards. He might be rebelling and may want more autonomy in his life. It may be that his self-confidence has taken a tumble for some reason, and he has become afraid of failing so is no longer trying. It is also quite possible that he has gotten too big for his britches and is pushing his luck.

Parents	Teachers
• Indicate that you are pleased to drop the use of rewards because you prefer to rely on trust.	• Reward systems have to be consistent throughout any school. If the system does not seem to work with individual students, think more deeply about the possible explanation. Consider the experience of colleagues and brainstorm potentially more effective and flexible approaches, such as making specific tasks easier or establishing a quiet place where a student can do homework with help from you or a colleague.
• Make clear your confidence that your son can and will deliver, for his own benefit and future.	
• If you need to, remind him, firmly, of any agreement and restate that you assume it will be adhered to.	
• Once he reaches the age of about ten, invite him to rehearse the arguments in favor of working and trying hard and applying himself to the task at hand. Also discuss the downside of letting things slip. Avoid hectoring and talking at him.	

You can rule either by counting heads or breaking them.

Boys will give their best effort when the atmosphere around them is emotionally uncluttered and they feel stimulated by a sense of personal growth, self-discovery, and autonomy. They can then learn and develop any interest or talent in freedom, with the watchful and supportive eye of their parents in the background. However, boys are unlikely to feel in command and free when they feel pushed and pulled by other people's targets or expectations.

People who experience little or no control over their lives tend to search for any remaining area to assert themselves and keep a grip. Everyone needs some private space, and this reaction is a survival response; likewise, every child needs a sense of agency to feel alive and worthwhile, or he may disappear into a pit of self-doubting depression or an identity void. Examples of typical responses to reassert control include developing food fads or disordered eating habits; exercise fanaticism; cheating, stealing, or lying; and becoming obsessive about routines and personal habits.

Parents	Teachers
• Make sure your son has a right to be heard and the chance to be understood.	• Make sure every boy has a right to be heard and the chance to be understood.
• Encourage active and appropriate participation and involvement at all times.	• Through having responsibility, children find out about themselves. Put boys in charge of as much of their learning and assessment as possible.
• He will make the effort when he knows he can say his piece and is respected.	

Chapter 9

Using Praise to Encourage Learning and Behavior

It would not be surprising if many readers turned to this chapter first. People often seek guidance when they feel things are going off the track. In terms of what is a common problem for parents, school performance and behavior are the two big ones. Praise, encouragement, and positive feedback are especially valuable and effective in these two areas. They are also far more likely to produce happier and more self-directed children than punishment, harsh criticism, or humiliation. But parents can find themselves in trouble, despite using a range of "positive" and recommended inducements, without really understanding why. It is for this reason that learning and behavior are addressed here, for it is important that parents know the general principles of effective praise (and some of the pitfalls of praise) before they seek answers to any immediate problem. It is also important to be clear about the best ways to get the best from our children.

But first, a few words about both learning and discipline. The better these are understood, the easier it will be for parents to keep feedback positive and constructive.

Learning is an emotional activity and a very complex process. It involves far more than a child's simply opening his mind and receiving knowledge because his *state* of mind inevitably influences his willingness and capacity to take in information. When children struggle at school there are often several complex explanations. Difficult life events, including bullying, can distress and preoccupy children so that they're unable to concentrate. These same events may threaten children's self-belief because they often introduce uncertainty and powerlessness, making children less willing to take the risks that learning entails. Learning can also arouse a range of fears: of incompetence, of failure, of reprimand and ridicule. Children are agents of their own learning. Rather than be forced to absorb information and then receive the "gift" of positive feedback, they can be offered the chance to decide and say *how* best they learn, *when* they are ready to pull out all the stops, and *whether* they need tokens of appreciation.

Discipline should also foster self-restraint and self-discipline. Boys shouldn't have adult requirements ruling all of their time. We set clear guidelines for them early on to keep them safe and secure. As they grow older, however, boys must be encouraged to judge situations for themselves and reflect on both the reasons for any disappointing behavior and the consequences—any harm or distress caused to property or people. Eventually, they must develop their own values and manage their own study patterns and behavior. Parents and others will encourage this self-discipline if they reward boys' reflection and responsibility and treat compliance more as an expectation.

Success is always relative

I had a greater sense of achievement from finishing 73rd in the national school championships aged fourteen than from coming sixth in the 10,000 meters in the 1972 Olympics, which I was expected to win. It was a disaster for me. But I tried to hang on to the positive view that I was sixth best in the world.

—David Bedford, British athlete who created the annual London Marathon

It is important to realize that what might be a small, unremarkable step forward for one boy can be a significant mark of progress for another, and a successful result for someone who needs to work hard to do well may be a disappointing one for someone else who rides challenges easily and is capable of better. No one should be denied his parents' pleasure just because someone with greater talent was in the lineup to outshine his personal effort.

In school, children are viewed as learners and are judged and differentiated by academic ability. At home, we must see our son in the round and as multitalented; always offer a sense of hope and help him develop the self-respect necessary to acquire a positive self-image even if academic excellence is not his strong point.

Parents	Teachers

- Every boy learns and develops in a different way and takes a different amount of time to do so. "He's a late developer" may be the truth, rather than a convenient, embarrassed cover-up response to skeptical friends or relatives.

- Remember that stressful experiences can put learning on hold. And all children need times when they tread water rather than surge forward.

- Ask your son whether completing a project felt good to him. If it did and he's not pretending, that's good enough.

- If your friends' children are doing "better" than yours, avoid feeling competitive. Yours are still lovable as they are.

- Consider each piece of work as a good or less good one *for them at this moment,* not in relation to the standard you ultimately expect.

- Whole-class praise is good from time to time so everyone feels the benefit.

72 | Match the applause to the achievement

> *Oh good job, Danny! I love how you are sitting quietly at the table! Everyone, put your hands together for a little clap!*

"Say it enthusiastically" is a mantra adopted by many parenting and management gurus and therefore by parents. Of course, it is undoubtedly better to sound pleased than to describe pleasure with a deadpan expression and a flat voice; however, the fervor espoused by many can go too far in the other direction and not only sound fake but also put too much pressure on a child to continue to receive the accolades.

If praise is about appreciation, and appreciation involves estimating the worth of something, we need to match the applause to the achievement.

Parents	Teachers
• Encouragement includes waiting quietly and patiently while a child works out how to do something. It shows trust that he'll manage.	• Ask a student how he would like a good piece of work acknowledged other than with your written comment, if at all.
• Saying something's great before it has been achieved is false and can imply there is pressure to get it right. However, showing appreciation of endeavor thus far suggests that that is good enough.	• Accumulate small achievements to justify a bigger splash of recognition. Three achievements in one week or in one semester could earn different rewards.
• Children feel pride and pleasure not when they receive phony feedback about their brilliance but when they know they have worked hard and have something significant to show for it.	• For young boys, a week, or even a day, is long enough. Older boys can relate to improvements over a longer period.

73 | Praise friendship and caring qualities, too

A UNESCO report, *International Commission on Education for the Twenty-first Century*, identified four kinds of learning: learning to know; learning to live together; learning to be; and learning to do.

Schools focus mostly on learning to know, and it is what boys know, or rather seem not to know, that upsets parents most. Yet friendship and caring qualities are also important, and if boys can work in collaboration with friends, they can gain great insight and broaden their awareness from pooling ideas and approaches.

Boys seem to have more finely honed competitive instincts and often prefer to work on their own instead of with classmates in order to gain some distinction. However, in the adult working world, teamwork is highly valued, so boys need to overcome their reluctance. At a time when it is important to their sense of masculinity to be successful and all-knowing, they may feel more exposed in group work because others will see if they can't grasp something or have no suggestions to contribute.

Parents	Teachers

- Having opportunities to work with friends, even if they gossip and seem to be off task some of the time, can benefit a boy's learning through enhancing his language and social and communication skills.

- Learning is inevitably a social activity. It never happens in a vacuum. It always involves listening, interacting with a teacher, responding to peers' and teachers' expectations and testing and reshaping "self" assumptions in the light of the reactions of others. Social confidence can encourage more confident work.

- If you have class awards, don't forget to acknowledge humor or other social attributes.

- Try to encourage boys to feel comfortable in group-based projects.

- "Groupthink" is greater than the sum of its parts. Demonstrate through an exercise that ideas can develop and strengthen when people work together.

My seven-year-old son enjoyed writing at home, creating well-punctuated, long stories. When he brought some schoolwork home, I was shocked at the contrast and how little care he'd taken. Instead of telling him off and pointing out his mistakes, I went to the teacher to discuss why he might be working so differently at school.

When young children are proud of something they have done, of course they want to show it to us. Rather than burst their bubble of confidence with critical comments, we should aim to appreciate the piece of work and accept that they are pleased with it. If we spot something wrong or something we feel could have been done better—as we're almost bound to, being adults—we have to think carefully about how and whether to say anything. It is essentially for the teacher, who knows the standard expected for our child's age, to do the teaching.

If our son asks us to check his work over, we can be more straightforward, but only after having first commented positively on something we liked about the work and having checked that he is ready to hear any suggestions for changes. Some children will be happy to dive back in; others may decide they will leave their work as it is, and this is their choice.

Parents	Teachers
• Get too critical, and your son won't let you near to help at all.	• Parents who complain are parents who care. Go easy on them, and try not to take it personally.
• Avoid changing anything or adding finishing touches as he'll no longer see the work as his.	• Guidance for parents on helping with homework issued at the start of the school year may help to set the groundwork for any future discussions.
• Only the teacher can know what to expect from a boy of his age, what is really being tested in the homework, and what's best for him to learn next.	
• If there is a big difference between what he produces at home and in class, consult rather than berate the teacher. The problem could be a boisterous friend, boredom, disruptive classmates, or feeling different if he does his best.	

75   Every day can't be judgment day

*I don't like to punish any boy in my class. If some-
one is failing and falling behind, I deal with it by
giving him personal attention. There is nothing like
a one-to-one session to help iron out difficulties and
make someone feel valued and hopeful. But I would
do it very quietly and not announce to the class that
this is what I felt was needed.*

If our bosses were to check us over each day and give
us daily marks out of ten, we'd end up ragged and neu-
rotic. That's how children must feel when they are
regaled with constant expressions of pleasure and disapproval. It's hard for them to find that necessary private
space when they feel they are being watched inces-
santly. One teenager told me it was his mother's carping
alternated with squeals of delight according to each
day's events that led him to clam up when she asked
what had happened at school.

Parents	Teachers
• Encouragement contains no judgment. It leaves your son free to take himself forward in his own way.	• Make earning any smiley stickers fun.
• Use encouraging comments to help him to feel you're appreciating rather than judging:	

• Use encouraging comments to help him to feel you're appreciating rather than judging:

— "You've put so much effort into that!"
— "I wish I'd done such interesting things at school."
— "It's hard for you but you will get it."

• Anticipate and remove any guilt or shame he might feel if he anticipates judgment: "That wasn't at all like you. Let's put it behind us and start again tomorrow."

76 | Show interest but don't be intrusive

One mom who had a very high-powered job said she was not going to attend the parent-teacher night at her son's school because she considered it the school's job to get the teaching right. She wasn't interested in hearing what she could do—that was what she was paying them for.

How wrong she was! Of course we should be interested in our child's progress and happiness in all areas of development at school. For all schoolchildren, school is almost as important as their family; for older children, it is probably more important.

But we have a dilemma. All children need some private space, and after the age of eight or so children relish school as the place where they can disappear from the often intense gaze of their parents' constant scrutiny. They need some privacy. Their need for praise from us becomes offset gradually by their need for autonomy. When boys want our appreciation, they'll tell us all we need to know.

Parents	Teachers
• Ask open-ended questions that allow your son to withhold detail: "Did anything good or bad happen today?" not "Who did you play with and what happened?" And start by talking about *your* day.	• Show interest in a boy's personal passions or hobbies, but step back if he seems uncomfortable about it.
• Ask casually about grades: "That tricky math test: How did it go?" rather than "What mark did you get? Will I be pleased?"	• His family experiences influence him a great deal. It is important to understand and acknowledge these, but also to treat anything you learn about him with respect, since many children prefer this information to remain private.
• If you overhear talk of a difficulty, offer to discuss it but don't demand details.	
• Make sure your questions are genuine, not designed to find out something else.	• At parent-teacher events and in newsletters, stress the important role that parents can play in encouraging their children in schoolwork and being interested in any developments in school.
• Take an interest in his work, but don't take it over and do it yourself.	

77 Give him hope

The road to a destination is as important as arriving there, and along the road there should always be hope. Most boys give up either because they have been told over and over that they are a hopeless case or because they doubt their capacity to do well for other reasons. The message many hear is demoralizing and undermining: "You won't if you don't . . . "; "You will never succeed if you carry on . . . "; or "You're a born loser; you've never been any good at . . . " Rather than risk further failure and have salt rubbed in their already wounded egos, many boys decide not to try. Labels tend to stick and act as straitjackets, preventing boys from escaping from the negative destiny that someone has assumed is in store for them.

What boys need to hear are far more hopeful messages that will not only boost their self-belief but also make any target seem manageable and easy to keep up once achieved; for example, "Of course this is hard, but just take it one step at a time and you'll have no problem." Or at the store, "You've managed to stay close and not run off from the vegetable section all the way to the meat. It's not so far now to the checkout. Did you think it would be this easy? I knew you could do it!"

Parents	Teachers

Parents

- Remind your son of past successes so he thinks positively and believes in himself.

- If success appears unfamiliar or scary and seems to carry heavy responsibilities for continuing in the same vein, it may be easier for a boy to remain the devil he knows.

- If he sets himself a goal that he's failed to complete before, such as to cover his bedroom wall with posters and photos from magazines, don't remind him of the past failure. Greet each resolution as a first and stay positive.

- Motivation is grounded in hope and experience.

Teachers

- Sarcasm and ridicule usually puncture hope. Don't use them.

- Make sure that a boy's hope is grounded in a practical reality. Help him to put together a plan.

- Break the challenge down into small, manageable chunks, and remind him of difficulties he has previously overcome.

78 Boys like to hold a bit back

Boys like to keep a bit of themselves back, so their work is rarely perfect. They like to take the short-cuts, prefer to answer their science questions in incomplete sentences, and not bother too much about neatness. We're used to that. I don't like to squeeze much more out of them if they've clearly understood the work.

These views were expressed by an experienced high school science teacher. Whether it relates to male pride or an extra sensitivity that boys have to power struggles with parents, boys can feel they give too much of themselves away when they do everything exactly as asked by an adult. Whether it is managing their bedrooms or behavior at home or their homework for school, boys like to persuade themselves that they're still in control, that they haven't sold their soul. Doing almost all of it, or doing it nearly right, is often as good as you're going to get.

Rather than force them to do it your way, it's better to accept that enough is, indeed, enough to accept and worthy of your appreciation.

Parents	Teachers
• Respect your son's differences. Don't try to take over his soul.	• Be understanding of work that's not quite what you had in mind, provided it is thought through, demonstrates learning, and is legible.
• Be tolerant. This "unfinished business" approach to many tasks may also reflect a boy's greater difficulty with concentrating for long periods of time.	• Avoid commanding total obedience in every way. Have a joke about minor stubbornness and male pride.
• Boys may need especially to create a protective moat between themselves and successful fathers who have high expectations of their sons. Respond with empathy rather than insisting that standards must not be allowed to slip.	

Learning anything is a strange business, for it rarely happens in a predictable way or to a set pattern. Children learn, mature, and develop in phases and spurts, and each one will manage it in his unique way. Boys get "eureka" moments when everything falls into place, but then they can get quite scared and may want to return to the time they were more dependent and needed to rely on help. That way, they do not risk being wrong. At each stage of the advance, they can feel quite exposed. Learning, therefore, is often a case of two steps forward, one step back, as the knowledge or new behavior starts to feel normal.

In relation to behavior, boys often need to test our reactions, to check that we really have become cooler, kinder parents and won't revert to being harsh or frightening if they slip up again. If parents ride the highs and lows because this is understood, this is a form of acceptance and affirmation that has the same effect as giving direct praise.

We may also witness "two steps back, three great leaps forward." Younger children may appear to go into reverse before they make a significant developmental advance—their brains seem to take a vacation before they go full speed ahead.

Parents	Teachers
• When a boy needs to tread water for a while and take time out from the pressure of eternal "progress," he should certainly not be frowned upon or punished.	• Curriculum targets and standardized tests assume that every child is developing as the "average," when each one actually progresses uniquely.
• If your son seems to have "lost it" and become confused or cannot do something he could before, wait patiently. Within a week it is likely he will have rediscovered the ability and made a significant advance.	• Try to include some flexibility in the study program. • Give a flagging boy confidence that he is not stupid, merely working on the problem in his way and at his own speed.
• Children learn by doing, but they also learn by sleeping on it, imagining it, "playing with" the idea, and thinking it through subconsciously. Don't ask for minute evidence of step-by-step learning.	• Try to convince him that he'll catch up, and impress on him that, like any investment, "past performance is no guarantee of future outcomes!"

At my son's parent-teacher meetings, a number of teachers said he could do better than he was doing at present. He was performing fine in his favorite subjects, so there was nothing wrong with his working habits or brain when he was fired up. But instead of asking him to do each teacher's bidding, I suggested that he apply extra effort to one subject each semester to keep it manageable. He felt no pressure, and his work gradually improved.

Boys tend to be active and busy, which means they can find it hard to concentrate on doing the right things for a whole day. They make lots of mistakes, and it is equally trying for us to monitor every move to ensure our son is obliging and obedient. He has someone constantly on his back, and our spying tactics imply that we expect transgressions and don't trust him.

Everyone benefits by picking on one aspect of behavior or schoolwork to turn around at a time. The chances of success are higher, the nagging and snooping decline, and life is more generally relaxed. Most valuable, once things have improved on the central problem, other challenging behavior tends to disappear as a result of fewer fights, less resentment, and a higher profile of praise and encouragement.

Parents	Teachers

- Identify the behavior that bugs you most or the time of day that is most trying, and start there. Drop the nagging about other problems until the top priority is sorted out.

- Let your son know that this is your plan, and make it seem like a fair contract: He does his bit and you do yours, which is staying cool about other matters.

- For schoolwork, suggest that he work to improve one subject at a time. Don't ask him to pull out all the stops on his reading and his math, or his science and his history, at the same time.

- With a challenging class, reflect upon the source of the main problem—a handful of particularly disruptive students, classroom management (because they sit and disrupt together), or teaching style (because some seem to lose interest very quickly). Pick the most plausible explanation, and unravel that problem first.

- Give boys who struggle clear and achievable short-term goals so they know exactly where they must focus and see the way forward. When one does well, make sure he knows exactly what he did that led to the improvement.

Chapter 10

The Perils of Perfectionism

Many people have become concerned that an increasing pressure to achieve and do well has led to more high-flying students becoming perfectionists and "success junkies," dependent on their regular fix of achievement and accolades, success and celebration, without which they feel incomplete. For example, the former dean of Harvard's undergraduate college, Harry Lewis, was openly concerned by some students' need to impress and to receive acknowledgment and rewards for everything when he wrote to these students, "You may balance your life better if you participate in some activities purely for fun. . . . Many of the most important and rewarding things that you do will be recorded on no piece of paper you take with you but only as imprints on your mind and soul."

Whereas some children seem able to survive, even thrive on, pressure, others may develop an unhealthy level of perfectionism that conceals considerable self-doubt and distress because they pursue often impossible goals and are never satisfied with the result.

What attitudes and support help to keep children free of turmoil and competitive anxiety? Research shows that children who aim high, do well, and can sustain success in a healthy and balanced way work toward their own, realistic, and flexible standards and expectations. They can ride mistakes and failures and learn from them. They tend to be well organized, to have uncritical parents, and to strive for their own benefit because they enjoy the activity. They are in control and don't feel pushed. Most important, they have a robust self-esteem that does not rely on proving themselves to others or coming out on top.

The seeds of unhealthy perfectionism take root where, in the eyes of the child, parental approval appears conditional on success; where children strive to meet very high and inflexible expectations that they see others hold for them; where adults take the credit for, or "steal," any success; where no success ever seems good enough because targets are continuously raised; where constant challenge generates constant doubt about ability; and where success is lauded and fear of failure is intense. In other words, perfectionist attitudes do not help children to be happy, despite the often impressive achievements that accumulate: Just one setback will suggest a whole future strewn with failure.

If parents overemphasize being successful from an early age, a boy may become obsessed with doing well because he believes his parents' approval depends on it. Constant striving reinforces his doubt that any success is good enough. This self-doubt and the associated anxiety may result in burnout or opting out—the opposite of what parents want! The tips in this chapter suggest how to help boys develop healthier attitudes toward both success and failure.

Keep all goals realistic and flexible

Everyone Gets Scars on the Way to the Stars
—Song title by Fran Landesman, jazz singer

Parents and teachers are often tempted to ask a child to go that extra mile and are loathe to make the target easier if the child then struggles. If a problem appears, it is attitude and application that are considered the culprit, not an unrealistic target.

Research shows that being able to be flexible and to compromise on standards and targets is one of the keys to healthy striving. If a boy begins to set tough targets and beats himself up emotionally if he doesn't quite get there, encourage him to go easy. Of course it's great if he does very well, but it is more important that he not find himself in a perfectionist straitjacket.

Parents	Teachers
• Never berate a boy for having not quite excelled, even as a joke.	• Boys need high expectations for meeting deadlines to prevent procrastination from becoming a habit, but they need flexible expectations when they have determined their own goal.
• Try to demonstrate flexibility in your own goal setting.	
• Don't harbor inflexible goals for your son.	
	• Make it clear that each student achieves at a different level, but that high performance should not come at the expense of enriching leisure time or peace of mind.

82 Don't make approval conditional on his success

When my son was not selected to be head of his school, I felt let down and almost angry. I got really picky with him. I found myself putting him down. I'm an intelligent and successful businessman and was both horrified and ashamed that I felt this way. It just happened.

At least this father admitted his feelings. His first reaction—of vindictive disappointment—is more common than anyone would care to accept, although his subsequent insight is far less usual. If we expect good things, it is very easy to feel disappointed and let down if they do not happen, but no child should suffer the burden of believing that success is the only way to maintain either his parents' love or their approval.

We might have a similar reaction if our son behaved badly on an occasion that mattered to us and we felt shown up. If we "went cold" on him but did not actually reprimand him for a specific wrongdoing, we could be falling into the trap of reserving our approval for times when he makes us feel good.

Parents	Teachers
• Accept that it is not good for your son to aim to be perfect, and that every experience, including a setback, is an important stepping-stone in learning and growing.	• Treat all students fairly, without favoritism. Accept each one as a worthwhile individual; don't reserve your enthusiasm for the accommodating and successful ones.
• See the funny side and the alternative potential of any shortfalls.	• Show that you value a wide range of attitudes, specialist knowledge, and skills. Refer to past achievements and anticipate future ones.
• If you find yourself being disappointed by a second-best outcome, it is time to remind yourself that you are not him, and he is not you. In your mind, draw a boundary between you and him and stop living through him.	• Focus on the process as well as the outcome. How the improvement was achieved is the aspect to highlight, rather than the success itself.
	• Encourage all students to make important decisions and take responsibility for these, so each one feels trusted by you.

83 Let your son take—and keep—ownership of the success

Children need to keep possession of any success and realize that it's theirs. No one should run off and tell the world, as if it was their achievement and their prize.

—Special educational needs
expert and head teacher

Of course, our son owns his success, but it is very easy to take it over and thereby take it from him. That is what we are doing when we use it to make us feel successful. We feel so thrilled by the achievement we are almost driven to run off with it and show it to all our friends by telling them. We can get enormous kudos when our children do very well in their various activities.

But if we effectively steal our son's success and spread around any special news, our son could be left feeling empty and bereft, rather than fulfilled. He could then feel driven to replenish the success, over and over again.

Parents	Teachers
• Personal success should be seen as the child's property, not the parent's. You would not consider borrowing anything of his without asking, and the same courtesy should apply here.	• When schools use children's achievements to pump up their standing, there is a danger that students will feel used.
• Check first whether he wishes anyone else to know, and if he would like to tell any particular person himself.	
• Asking him not only shows you respect him and his wishes, but also makes the success unambiguously his.	
• Devaluing something that is a success in his terms is another way of taking the achievement and pleasure away from him: "But a third of the class got that mark. That's not so special!"	

Don't be arrogant enough to assume you always know what a boy wants and how he feels. It is important to keep talking. Give him the opportunity to discuss freely his fears and feelings, including those that could hurt or disappoint you.

He must be free to talk about shame, his fear of failure, letting you down, or wanting to do some activity other than the one you have encouraged. There will be pluses to discuss, too, such as which aspects of his life give him the most pleasure and how he rates each of his talents or particular skills.

For example, if we celebrate a child's success, the event should suit him, not us. A ten-year-old could find it hard to relate to a horde of neighbors or relatives descending on his home, talking to each other, and enjoying alcohol. If he is shy, as is likely, he'll probably sneak off to his room—so what benefit is the gathering to him?

Parents	Teachers

- Plan the celebration at your son's level, not how you would mark something notable that happens to you.

- Take his worries seriously. Don't ignore something that saddens him.

- If we refuse to see things his way, he could lose touch with himself and become merely a reflection of us.

- Younger children readily believe in the unbelievable, such as Santa Claus and tooth fairies. They make sense of things in surprising ways. Just because we know why something has to be as it is, it does not follow he also understands.

- Try to uncover any worries that lie behind late, "lost," or very poor work. There could be distress at home, or the student could fear demonstrating his total lack of understanding, and so he doesn't bother at all.

- Appreciate that strong parental antagonism toward school and study could dilute a boy's commitment to work, and he's likely to struggle with the conflict.

85 | Talk about "development," not "improvement"

Boys who have the opportunity to discover new interests, talents, and skills learn more about themselves and establish a pattern of self-discovery that can enrich the rest of their lives. Alongside enjoyment, self-discovery is a key benefit of pursuing interests: Only if children explore what is there inside them can they discover their true potential and experience the thrill and excitement that lies in store. The process should be one of self-development, not self-improvement.

Self-improvement implies that a boy is progressively better and more clever than he was before. It suggests that how he was before was not "right"; yet, to repeat, he needs to see his past as an acceptable part of him. We should not demand that he "fulfill his potential," because we can never know what potential is there or when it is fulfilled. Better to ask him to unpeel a layer or two of possible resistance to reveal his reserve of capability—for his own enjoyment.

Parents	Teachers
• Make it clear that it is the results or the technique that is improving, not his personality or "self."	• Separate the boy from the improvement. Talk about his understanding deepening, his application becoming more effective, or his skill growing rather than marveling at his "improvement."
• Talk about discovery, rather than improvement: "You're discovering all sorts of new things about yourself!" "You're discovering you can feel comfortable with math after all"; "Did you think you could speed up your sprint time so successfully?"	

Encourage self-appraisal

Society has told boys for a very long time that they must ultimately manage on their own and the sooner they start, the better—for so long, in fact, that it could now be programmed into their brains. Boys are proud. They don't always want to do everything they are told, especially if it is mothers and female teachers doing the telling. From the start of the preteen years and well into adolescence, boys have a tendency to disparage girls and women, to establish a clearer masculine identity. If praise is not transmitted carefully, even that can be viewed with suspicion as a tool of manipulation.

The best tactic with boys is to encourage self-appraisal. Facing their strengths and weaknesses head on will not only increase realism and self-knowledge but also prevent typically male "posturing." It also takes the power out of praise. Parents can nonetheless offer positive support, either by reinforcing their son's individual judgments or by reflecting encouragingly at the end of the week. Of course, if he has a significant "victory," we can be more spontaneously appreciative.

Parents	Teachers
• Ask, "But what did you think of it? That's the more important test because you are the best judge."	• Some teachers invite their students to moderate each other's work, having first discussed what points, skills, and understanding needed to be covered. The judgment any boy applies to another's work will be fresh to apply to his own.
• Try to encourage your son to be specific: "You said you thought you did badly. What was it that didn't go right?" or, "Yes, I liked what you did, too. What pleased you in particular?"	• Ask any boy who you feel is widely misjudging the standard expected how he responds to your comments on any assignment.
• Such details become the checkpoints for assessing the accuracy or relevance of his judgment.	
• Before his report card is due, ask him for his best guess of what will be included.	

87 Don't constantly move the goalposts

My four-year-old son was well prepared for his inoculations at the pediatrician's, so much so that he didn't cry at all. Amazed at such maturity, the clinician decided to give the second dose at the same time. The result was traumatic: a distressed and disconsolate child who felt let down by both mother and doctor.

Demanding schools and parents are prone to move the goalposts. As soon as one target is in sight and therefore appears easy, another, more challenging one is presented to prevent any flagging of effort. Or as soon as one goal has been reached, another is put in place to maintain the momentum: "If you can achieve that, then surely this is also within reach!"

But boys like to decide when they will undertake challenges. They have become used to computer games in which they select the level of difficulty and start again as a "beginner" in a higher level only when top scores at a previous level fail to please. It is very empowering.

Parents	Teachers
• Challenges must tempt boys to discover themselves, not threaten them, put them off, or make them feel inadequate until they fulfill them.	• Factor in the child's view of what he can achieve and put him in control as much as is practical to reduce the pressure.
• When boys take their own time to select the target, their readiness reflects their confidence.	• Asking for perfect answers before moving someone on encourages perfectionist attitudes.
• Shifting goalposts represent a broken deal. Boys can store up resentment, self-doubt, and anxiety.	

88 | Accept good-enough success

My father never let me rest. Nothing ever seemed quite good enough for him. The B team wasn't, in either winter or summer sports—and he came to watch my matches and shout embarrassingly from the side until I was 18. It wasn't enough to play one instrument, it had to be two, and I had to be in all the available school bands and orchestras. He made me do jumping jacks every morning because he thought my co-ordination wasn't good enough. No wonder I have found it hard to relax and do anything just for fun.

—Peter, age 20

Carrying on from the previous tip: Any boy faced with successive mirage-style targets—ones that disappear as you approach, like the apparently shimmering "pools" of water on hot roads on sunny days—will very likely conclude that no success is good enough. If no success, however great, is good enough, a child will never know if he is good enough or, indeed, if he is any good at all. This is a very uncomfortable thought, so he will need to achieve more success to convince himself that he is good enough and worthy of praise. Success, if sought for this reason, will not raise self-esteem or self-belief, nor will it deepen the self-concept. At worst, it deepens self-doubt; at best, it leaves someone's self-esteem vulnerable and prone to fluctuation.

Self-belief does not come from a sense that we are perfect but from the knowledge that we are good enough and have more to give.

Parents	Teachers

- Lead your son when he's ready. For success to benefit self-worth, a boy needs time to absorb the achievement, to be sure he can repeat it, and to make it part of his identity. Only he can know when he is ready.

- Being pushed to move on too soon generates considerable anxiety, a noted characteristic of perfectionists, who feel driven by others.

- Good-enough success is not a cop-out and does not mean accepting second best or laziness. It is the result of honest (though perhaps not top-gear) striving that produced real progress and is the guard against either internal or external pressure.

- Let all success be good enough, at least for a time, including your own.

- Ask your students when they are ready to make an extra push to raise their grades or enter a competition.

- Untidy work can be considered good enough if the content is sound. Find out why the work was apparently rushed; if it was to create time to fit in other valuable activities, it could be a sensible trade-off.

> *A Washington investigation in 2000 claimed 20 percent of college students take illegally the behavior-modifying drug Ritalin to improve their concentration and performance.*

Some researchers contend that boys begin life more inclined to take risks than girls. They tend to think ahead less, so are less cautious: They can jump straight into things, get into more scrapes, and therefore end up being scolded more than girls. This bravado encourages boys to leave things to the last minute, protected by their conviction that "it'll go just fine on that night."

The ability to take risks is important, for learning is a risky business. Coming down hard when a boy has risked something and got it wrong or, even worse, punishing that error could lead him to avoid taking any risks.

Boys with perfectionist tendencies set very high standards for themselves. Fear of falling short tempts some to self-handicap to avoid anxiety, consciously or unconsciously. A boy may procrastinate, aim ridiculously high to ensure failure, or aim too low so the result means nothing. Some boys develop inexplicable lethargy, strange pains, or eating disorders, any of which provide a welcome excuse to exit the proverbial rat race.

Parents	Teachers
• Make it safe to make mistakes.	• If you make a mistake, be open and honest about it.
• Talk honestly about any mistakes you might have made in the past and any you make now.	• Raise class awareness of differing attitudes toward mistakes by initiating a discussion. Observe any gender patterns, and talk about them.
• If you have taken a risk in any field, discuss with your son why, what was the downside, and whether and how it paid off.	• Boys love class games and quizzes in which they can prove their cleverness—or expose their limitations. Girls are often too timid to enjoy them. Invite students to reflect upon what winning, losing, or participating means to them.
• Adventurous play that incorporates a measure of planned risk or that confronts the unexpected is helpful to learning.	
• Promote self-direction. Don't become so involved and protective that your son is never exposed to risk and therefore becomes risk-averse.	• Boys with low self-belief have neither the courage to take chances nor the confidence to change.

90 Don't ignore or punish failure

Parents are often advised to encourage children by ignoring mistakes and focusing on what they do well. This approach helps very young boys, who find it hard to control their bodies and feelings, take the first steps in learning. However, as they mature, they should be honest about the quality and effect of their work and behavior. To continue to disregard failures while celebrating successes suggests that failure is shameful and must be avoided, a view typical of perfectionists.

Failure is not something to be shunned. It provides factual and neutral information on what went wrong, what has not been understood fully, and what needs to be changed next time. The experience of failure becomes shameful to a child only when he has invested his self-worth in doing well, or when parents rely on a son's success for their own sense of satisfaction and happiness.

Parents	Teachers
• Respond sensitively to setbacks. Neither punishment nor trivialization is a helpful reaction to disappointments.	• Boys can see failure as a challenge to their masculine power and dominance. Help to take the shame out of any failure and clarify the lessons to be learned.
• Help your son to take responsibility for any failure. Make him move beyond the cover of feeble excuses to be clear about what went wrong.	• Hear a boy's side of the story.
• See failure as neutral, and don't rub his nose in it or tease him. Discourage him from taking it too personally.	
• Making mistakes can show he is working at the frontier of his knowledge and understanding, so be tolerant.	
• If his failures become your personal shame or his successes lift you from gloom, you make it harder for him.	
• Fortify his heart, don't thicken his skin.	

Chapter 11

Praise and You

Having spoken to countless adults over the years, to people who have been successful as well as those leading less remarkable lives, I have found it surprising how many were quick to volunteer that their parents, and particularly their fathers, never praised them. They never felt their efforts were appreciated and were left with a feeling that they were simply not good enough or not sufficiently interesting personalities to be noticed. This self-assessment has influenced the course of the lives of some, for they are still trying to please even though the parent is no longer around to watch the show. They continue to have unfinished business, and although this urge may lead to higher achievement than a more contented childhood might have delivered, the success masks an eternal sadness, a sense of letdown, and an underlying restlessness.

One acquaintance, who is now a leading politician and active in government, agreed that her desire to prove herself as good as her brothers in the eyes of her father sparked her need to make a mark from a young age. One man who sits at the top of his profession readily acknowledged the importance of self-esteem and said he had suffered quietly all his life because his father had neither praised him nor appeared to recognize or value his talents. As a consequence, he was happy now to be able to work with young students and graduates to encourage them to strengthen their sense of self through acquiring wider experiences of which they could feel proud.

Someone who experienced difficulty at the other end of the range of parental behavior is a young woman who showed early musical talent and was expected to meet demanding practice and performance schedules and to make music her career. She was praised, but grudgingly and with conditions attached. Her success was never good enough. She felt increasingly that her life was not her own and that the only way to regain control was to give up. From that day on, she never touched her instrument again.

It is surprising that so many people have been so honest, for adults more commonly deny the importance of the things they weren't lucky enough to have or, alternatively, state that something potentially unpleasant that did happen had no lasting ill effect. The conclusion has to be that the impact on children, young or old, of living either without parental recognition or with parents who push too hard is clearly profound: It is a pattern that we should ensure is not repeated in the next generation.

91 | Unblock your blocks to giving praise

Many people find it very hard to give praise. Some feel uncomfortable using the unfamiliar words; some simply do not know what to praise; and others are deeply skeptical of the whole process. The most common reasons people give to justify being sparing with praise include:

- that it can easily make a boy bigheaded;
- that praise should be given only for "excellence," that is, outstanding achievement and effort beyond expectation;
- that if something could be better, it should not be praised as this praise could encourage laziness and send the wrong message about general standards and expectations;
- that a boy should do well in every sphere before he gets rewarded, in case he should take a slide in an activity a parent thinks really matters;
- that parents think they created the success, not the boy, because they suggested the study regime, for example, or paid for extra tuition;
- that previously praise has had no impact, so they drop it.

Fathers especially can be keen to maintain an edge over a son and may be slow to praise his academic or other success if it rouses jealousy or threatens male authority and pride.

Parents	Teachers
• Reflect on your childhood experiences and your current attitudes on giving and receiving praise. What has been your strongest influence?	• Reflect on your past, at home and at school, and ponder on any patterns you could be repeating.
• Think hard to detect any difference in your treatment of girls and boys.	• Consider whether you find it easier to respond encouragingly in the classroom or at home with your own family, and think through why it might be so.
• If you work outside the home, how do you praise people at work, if at all? Do you have the same approach at home? If not, why not?	
• Give as you receive. When your son shows you affection and regard (both can be considered praise), make sure you reciprocate.	

92   Ask for praise if you want to hear it

If you do not receive much positive feedback from your family, at work, or from your friends, it is likely that you have learned to do without it. Men tend to be more self-sufficient—or like to consider themselves so—and may not even notice its absence. Women are more praise-hungry in childhood and are also more likely to miss getting pats on the back as an adult.

If you want to hear it, ask for it; most "significant others" are willing to be supportive once they realize that partners or friends want some backup. Very few will refuse. Children can be encouraged to be appreciative after you have done something well, not just to be polite but as a genuine recognition of the special effort or achievement.

Those who think they can do without praise and consider it a big fuss about not very much will almost certainly find it harder to offer praise to others. They may think that boys, especially, should learn to grow up less needy of other people's approval. The best way to encourage a reluctant partner to become freer with his or her appreciation toward a child of yours is to take a back route and praise and appreciate the partner overtly first.

Parents	Teachers

- Be specific. Analyze what you'd like to have more of, for example, appreciation of your efforts or talents or acceptance of your views and values. Then go and ask for it.

- Children tend to take what is done for them, at any level, as "normal parenting." It's hard for them to see that less might be done for them, so don't be harsh about their apparent insensitivity.

- It is healthier to do something because you want to (in which case perhaps you don't need big thanks) rather than because you want to curry favor. But if you'd like your efforts appreciated, describe that bit extra that you gave. Genuine thanks grow from genuine giving.

- Think which job you think you do well and whose appreciation you would value. Then go and seek confirmation and reinforcement.

- Positive feedback can come from colleagues, line managers, students, and parents. How might each of these show their appreciation? What might you be entitled to expect?

93 | If you did something well, believe it

In a world that seems obsessed with excellence, especially achievements that deliver big financial rewards, it can be hard to feel any pride in less obvious successes—or to realize that is what they are despite their modest scale.

People at their work are increasingly being encouraged to identify and acknowledge their strengths and achievements. These might be relatively minor, such as responding sensitively to a junior member of the staff who came in with a problem but left with a lighter step and a plan of action. In the home environment, there's no boss to offer compliments on your efforts that day, no daily target to meet. But we have good moments and successes nonetheless, and there are hundreds of tasks to be done, with or without our children, that involve the same efficiency skills, conflict resolution, stress management, practical and communication and listening skills that are on show in the workplace.

Looking at what we did and did well (rather than at what we did not do) and feeling pleased about it will act as a boost and help us to be positive and encouraging with our sons and partners.

Parents	Teachers
• An appreciative child is one who smiles, is happy, and shows affection to you. And sometimes he actually says thanks.	• If you receive good feedback from a colleague, a senior manager, a parent, or a student about something you have done, accept that it is valid. Don't squirm and claim you did not deserve the affirmation or it was uncalled for because you did what you did in the line of duty.
• If you feel uncomfortable receiving praise, learn simply to say thank you and hold onto it; don't bat it back.	

If you think you have done something impressive, either given your starting point or because it represents a significant step toward a long-term goal, reward yourself. Whatever is your special treat, allow yourself to have it or do it.

The reward can be something you enjoy alone, or it could be something you choose to share with another person. It might be sitting down with a trashy book, watching a film or DVD during the day, taking a scented bath, having a drink with a friend, or watching the sports channels all day one weekend.

Marking an achievement with a reward helps you to acknowledge that you got there, so you are entitled to take a break; it proves that you are not compelled always to go that one step farther before you allow yourself to feel pleased; and it enables you to understand how your children might also value each small gesture of appreciation and feel their effort was worthwhile.

Parents	Teachers

Parents

- Think of things you might enjoy doing in any spare time, such as taking a walk or spending time in the garden. Remember these when you feel you deserve a treat.

- The best reward is your own satisfaction; then there are no "ifs" and "buts" floating around in your head. Practice saying to yourself, "Well done! I can be really pleased about that."

- Rewards don't always have to benefit you. You can share a treat or treat someone else if that gives you pleasure.

Teachers

- Reflect on the times during an inevitably pressured day that you might enjoy some respite when you feel you deserve it.

- Remember good-enough success. Making a special effort, even if things didn't go entirely as planned, is worth marking; otherwise, you might not try again!

95 Accept any praise given to you

If someone praises you, accept the praise and hold onto it. Don't squirm with discomfort or hand it back as soon as you can with the words, "It was nothing very special," "I'm not sure what I've done to deserve a comment like that," or "I was going to do it anyway." Girls and women are particularly prone to such self-denigration. They may have tried hard, but they usually believe that they should have done that anyway, which makes the effort seem commonplace, not worthy of comment.

If you often feel you don't deserve any recognition or accolades and instead you feel embarrassed when someone tells you you have done well, you may imagine that others feel the same, including your child. This makes it more likely that you will be sparing with your praise, to protect him from the expected discomfort.

But this reticence is not helpful. Far better to change your mind-set and learn to accept positive feedback with good grace when you are fortunate enough to receive it!

Parents	Teachers
• Practice saying thank you when you are given praise, and teach your boy to do the same.	• If any student says, "That was fun!" or "That was interesting," respond with a thank you rather than "Good". His comment is intended as complimentary feedback, not to make you realize he enjoyed it.
• Don't make a joke about giving or hearing praise until everyone in the family knows that, mostly, your praise is given straight and can be trusted. Only then is it safe to lighten things with a bit of fun, and then only on the odd occasion.	

Don't compete with your son

My father was so competitive with me. He would always have to beat me at chess, even when I first started playing, and claim he knew more than I did about anything. I felt he needed to take the pleasure out of my passions. From the age of eleven, I rode a bike to school, and sure enough he took it up as weekend exercise. When I took up running, you can imagine the so-called fun competitions he arranged to prove he could run faster. It was so sad and probably meant he felt very insecure, but during my childhood I felt he could never be proud of me. It also made it hard to be proud of myself.

—William, age 17

Avoid competing with your son. Some mothers and fathers find it hard to give their children the space to become better than, more good-looking than, or more skilled than themselves. But growing boys need to feel respected for their achievements, not constantly pushed into a parent's shadow.

Parents	Teachers

- Becoming competitive is more likely to discourage your son than to spur him to greater effort, as it could make him feel overpowered and dejected.

- Let him, sometimes, be better than you. "I am so impressed" is a good message to convey.

- If you are competitive with him, he's more likely to be so with others.

- Avoid referring to your past to claim any superior edge; you will almost certainly not have remembered the time or event accurately.

- "Know-it-all" students may become irritating, but never try to trip them up with difficult questions or be tempted to beat them in a competitive exchange of knowledge.

97 | Model respect for women

A father or father figure can help a boy to do well not just by praising him but also by expressing his respect for the professionalism of any female teacher, coach or carer, family friend or relative, and, naturally, his mother. Hearing upbeat and supportive views about their capabilities, specialist knowledge, and personal characteristics will help a boy to feel comfortable learning and taking advice from women.

This is especially valuable when he becomes more gender-aware and possibly antagonistic to girls and older females—usually sometime between the ages of eight and ten. Boys will do better and do themselves greater justice if they are able to distance themselves from macho culture, which tends to present masculinity as necessarily powerful and aggressive and superior to anything female, which is seen to be tainted with weakness.

Verbal or physical abuse or intimidation of his mother can also severely damage a boy's self-esteem, mental health, and future chances in life.

Parents	Teachers

- Parents need to earn their son's respect as he matures and becomes more discriminating. He will watch how well both parents treat each other and also other people and then decide whether they deserve his respect.

- Watch your words and reactions as you watch movies or television together. Swearing, catcalls, and derogatory remarks imply disrespect.

- Boys won't respect women if their mothers don't respect themselves and if they allow their sons to exploit them or be rude. Enforcing house rules that protect your interests are a first step.

- Every school should adopt sexual harassment and antidiscrimination policies. Female staff should, of course, treat their male colleagues with the same respect.

- Gender awareness and equality of regard should apply throughout the school and in every lesson.

98   Enjoy your own company and that of others

The best thing about having friends is that you can assume they spend time with you because they enjoy your company. If they didn't, they wouldn't. They let you know that you are good to be around, which at times can be quite intoxicating—and of course they are also there to share your problems if you ever need them, as well as to provide a source of great fun.

Enjoying the company of your friends will help you to realize why it is good to enjoy the company of your son. It will help him to feel valued and appreciated. It will also make him feel that he is someone who is able to give other people pleasure rather than to be a source of disappointment and strife, and it will provide an enormous boost to his confidence. If you give time to your friends and also show that you value and enjoy your son because you reserve time for him, he will get the true measure of the value you attach to him. Maintaining friendships therefore offers a double benefit, provided your friends don't crowd your son out.

Parents	Teachers
• "I've had a lovely morning with my friends, and now I'm having a lovely time with you. Aren't I lucky?"	• Enjoy your students by talking to them as you see them around the building between classes.
• If you take your son with you when you meet friends, make sure he feels involved, either in the group or with something you take for him to do.	• Take time to enjoy yourself with colleagues in the staff room rather than working continuously.
• Be careful if you collect your younger children from school that they don't feel ignored as they emerge because you are deep in conversation with others. Greet your children warmly each time.	
• Enjoyment occurs when we engage with the present, the here and now.	

99 Endorse yourself

Children reap dividends when parents are comfortable with themselves. This entails accepting personal histories and the decisions that have been made, or not made, in earlier years. We should not continue to beat ourselves up for anything that happened in the past or pretend that certain events did not happen. The more content we feel with ourselves, the less we will be tempted to relive or deny things through our children, and the more we will be able to support and encourage them in healthy ways that reflect and give space to their true selves.

If we think we are not valuable or that nothing we do is ever good enough, it is tempting to fill the emptiness that we feel inside with our son's successes or failures, and it is too easy to fashion an identity based on those and to mold him to suit. If we don't feel good enough, we are likely to be more demanding of success and more grudging in giving praise, waiting until we feel it is really deserved. If he makes a mistake, we could feel it as a reflection on us and may therefore either undervalue the importance of the event or criticize him to protect our self-image.

Parents	Teachers
• Write down your strong points.	• Write down your professional strengths, and enjoy and cherish these attributes.
• Identify your regrets. But every cloud has a silver lining; nothing is ever a total disaster. For every decision or event in the past that you regret, try to identify a positive personal trait or outcome that arose from it.	• List your weaker traits and consider how much they genuinely set you back.
	• Consider how much you pressure your students to cover up your feared weaknesses.
• Think of everything you have done to help others. Achievement is not just scored by publicly accepted measures.	• Try to accept that school should help students to thrive academically and socially and to mature in many ways. Recall instances when you have helped a student cope and develop, not just pass his exams.

Encourage yourself

Good parenting is not about perfection; it is impossible to get it absolutely right all the time. In any case, people differ in their views about what is the right, or best, response to any situation, so perfection is not a practical goal. We make mistakes as parents—lots of them—just as our growing boys do. We need encouraging pats on the back for doing our best: for trying new and more positive ways to say things to our sons; for trying to understand more about how they think and learn, and about parent-child dynamics—just as boys need encouragement. Our intentions and efforts are important, and these are often enough to bring about noticeable changes in our sons' attitude and performance that we need to acknowledge to help us continue our efforts to be more positive and supportive.

The future must look enticing. We are doing well enough, and we can make changes to make the future look rosier. Our boys can and will do well, and we should help them to imagine and expect a positive future by creating an atmosphere of hope for, belief in, and appreciation of everyone in the family in the here and now.

- Setbacks are normal—part of the ebb and flow of life. The future will be bright, and we will feel more encouraged if we try some of the tips in this book.

- Don't beat yourself up: Apply to yourself the recommended 4:1 praise to criticism or blame ratio. Every time you think you fall short, find four things to do or that you have already done that you can feel pleased about.

- "True power does not reveal itself" (Foucault, French philosopher). The healthy way forward is to provide a home in which each individual is empowered and able to explore his or her potential, quirks, and interests without pressure and intrusive guidance.

- Teaching is part of your life, but not all of it. Think of all the other ways to accept and evaluate yourself—community or faith activist, parent, partner, son or daughter—and be positive about your overall contribution.

- Be encouraged. The future is almost always rich and rosy if you open yourself to opportunities and think positively!

Postscript

In case you have reached the end of the book and feel a little swamped and confused by the "oughts" and "buts," having read it straight through, here are some suggestions and summaries.

In the broad view, far more children suffer today from not being praised enough than are being damaged by excessive or misplaced praise. Children have a profound need not only to be noticed by the close adults in their life but also to be affirmed, appreciated, and enjoyed. Spending time with children can be difficult when everyone is so pressured, but all efforts to do so will be amply rewarded with warmth and love from a child who feels secure, loved, and self-confident and wants to have fun as well as do well.

It is said that we remember a maximum of 10 percent of what we hear or read at any one time. Having been faced with one hundred tips and many more bullets, you might find it helpful to order your thoughts by writing down ten things that have remained clear and on which you could take action. Select some for a "good things to do" list and some for a "best avoided" group. Prioritize these, put them into practice for a few days, and then dip into the book again to expand your repertoire from these experiences. Some will work for you, some may not. The important guidance is to use strategies that you feel comfortable with, provided, of course, your son responds well to them and there are happy results all around.

Other books in this series available from
Da Capo Lifelong Books by
Elizabeth Hartley–Brewer

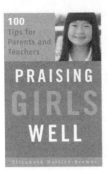

Praising Girls Well
ISBN 0-7382-1022-6
(978-0-7382-1022-3)

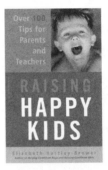

Raising Happy Kids
ISBN 0-306-81316-5

Raising a Self-Starter
ISBN 0-306-81315-7

Raising Confident Boys
ISBN 1-55561-320-9

Raising Confident Girls
ISBN 1-55561-321-7

For more information, visit www.dacapopress.com.